EVERYWOMAN'S MONEY BOOK

EVERYWOMAN'S MONEY BOOK

BETTY JANE WYLIE
LYNNE MACFARLANE

KEY PORTER BOOKS

Canadian Cataloguing in Publication Data

Wylie, Betty Jane, 1931-
   Everywoman's money book

Bibliography: p.
Includes index.
ISBN 0-919493-15-7

1. Women — Canada — Finance, Personal
I. MacFarlane, Lynne, 1932-   II. Title.

HG 179.W94 1984   332.024   C84-098166-X

Published by
Key Porter Books
59 Front Street East
Toronto, Ontario
M5E 1B3 Canada

Designed by Donald Fernley

Printed and bound in Canada

Contents

1. The Politics of Money *7*
2. Money Therapy *21*
3. Women and Credit *29*
4. Banking *37*
5. Borrowing *45*
6. The Budget *51*
7. Savings *63*
8. Insurance *73*
9. Retirement *83*
10. Investments *93*
11. Your Portfolio *107*
12. Real Estate *119*
13. Children and Money *131*
14. Estate Planning and Property Settlement *139*
15. Record Keeping and Income Tax *149*
16. As Beautiful As Roses *163*

Appendix — Division of Assets *171*
Glossary *187*
Additional Reading *200*
Index *203*
Acknowledgements *208*

To our daughters

1

The Politics of Money

"If you have no money, be polite."
DANISH PROVERB

The Fate of Canadian Women

If you're a woman living in Canada, odds are you're going to be poor at some time in your life — let's hope the time is already past.

We have a tendency to think that other women are poor because they are unfortunate, because they deserve it, because they are low-class and/or uneducated. We should think again. Three out of every five poor adults in Canada are women, according to a report on women and poverty by the National Council of Welfare. "Women are poor because poverty is a natural consequence of the role they are still expected to play in our society." And the reason they still play that role is that they grew up, as we did, with the dream of marrying Prince Charming and living happily ever after. And that meant being taken care of for the rest of their lives. Forget it.

"The foundation of the great financial vulnerability of women is the belief that most of them will always have a father or a husband on whom they can count," the report goes on. That belief is no longer justified by the facts. Nowadays, Prince Charming either turns back into a frog (two out of four marriages end in divorce) or else he croaks (there are a million widows in Canada). "Almost three out of every four women will find themselves on their own sometime in their adult lives. . . . Most poor women who live alone are over the age of 55." Two-thirds of single women over the age of 65 (single, for whatever reason — widowed, divorced, never married) live below the poverty line. We have seen the future, and it is bleak.

Women's Attitude to Money

That's one of the reasons we wrote this book. Women don't have to expect to be poor. There are things they can do to avoid it, and it's about time. This book is for women who know a little about money (it's nice to have) and want to know a lot more, who like the feeling of competence and confidence that knowing what they're doing with their money gives them. We all want to do more than pay our bills and keep afloat. We want to learn how to make money work for us rather than have to work so hard for our money and see it disappear.

It's not easy. Men are still better paid than women, so women have less money to put to work. It's said that the real wealth is in the hands of women, but that's a male myth. The *spending* may be done by the women — spending on food and household goods. The *investing* of the money is still largely in male hands. "Don't you worry your pretty little head about that" has been a smarmy way of telling us to keep our hands off the filthy stuff.

Older women often have no idea how to pay their household bills, no inkling what a credit rating is, no plans for their future, no awareness of the need for such plans. Younger women all too often consider their work a job and not a career. Even in this day and age, when they can look forward to working most of their adult lives, with time off (and this is optional now) for babies, these women, too, while they give some thought to their futures, still regard the middle distance and can't envision the distant future when they will be old and grey and full of sleep and very, very poor.

We like to think that that can't happen to women today, that the feminist movement, with its cry of equal pay for work of equal value and its claims for human rights, has made deep inroads into the public (read male) consciousness. Not so. It's another myth, and a popular one, that woman's lot has improved since Betty Friedan's first manifesto, *The Feminine Mystique*, was published in 1963.

Women and the Labour Force

"In spite of the dramatic rise in the labour-force participation of women in the last ten years," according to the *Women and Poverty* report, "the proportion of female workers occupying low-paying, clerical, sales and service jobs has remained unchanged." Today, two out of three women aged 24 to 55 are in the labour force, but many are still working in a narrower range of jobs, and at lower-paid jobs, than men. According to Statistics Canada's 1981 census, the average income gap

8

between males and females is $8,504. Nor does the gap close for women with university degrees. The census showed a difference of $13,635 between average incomes for females and males with degrees.

The Canadian Widow

The woman who has never worked and is widowed later in life, but with years yet to live, is also not only disappointed but cheated. The average amount of life-insurance death benefits paid out in 1977 was about $4,000. The average age at which a woman is widowed in Canada is 56. She has nine years to wait before she cuts into the Old Age Pension, which is also pegged below the poverty line. Not even a gold watch for faithful service. Being educated and being deserving are no protection for women from poverty.

What Does Money Buy?

So who's going to look after you? You are. But it isn't going to be easy. Right off the top, you have to change your attitude to money. Women tend to think of money as a preserver and a comforter, not, as men do, as a power tool. Money buys shelter, food, clothing, education and security. Of course that's true. But money also buys money, when it's used properly. It can be made to work.

Most women believe in cash, not credit. Most women are afraid of spending money, especially money they don't have. Unless they can see it, they don't believe it exists. That's because, as financial writer Paula Nelson puts it, "society still traditionally assigns to women the role of money-handler rather than money-maker." Therefore, even when women look after all the household accounts, they still may not be aware of the necessity of long-range financial plans — for that matter, their husbands may not be, either. In the past, a woman's idea of money management may have been to shop the specials, turn down the heat to cut the fuel bills and sew her own clothes. Now she's taking over the financial planning.

Women and Debt

Most women are terrified of debt. They like to pay their bills immediately, so no one will be mad at them, or bug them. The idea of creative debt — or borrowing — is alien to them. And the fact that they do not exist on paper (that is, that they have no credit rating because they have never been in debt) is astounding. Responsible citizens pay their bills promptly, and most women are determined to be responsible citizens. And they are. Surveys have shown that women

9

pay their bills more promptly and welsh on fewer debts than men do. That's because they're afraid of what might happen if they don't.

Women are Afraid of Ownership

Everyone is afraid of ownership, to a certain extent. A friend of ours remembers her husband's sleeplessness the first few nights they were in their first house. He had a mortgage — the largest amount of money he had ever owed — and he was scared. But our society has programmed men to accept these pressures and challenges. Now women have to program themselves and learn to accept the challenge and responsibility of ownership, among other things. We know a widow who was left quite comfortably, thank you, but who was afraid to buy a condominium after she sold her house. She is now being forced to buy one because the building she lives in is converting from rental to ownership terms. She is still scared about it — all that money! Fear of ownership, that's what it is.

So when it comes to owning stocks or bonds, what women tend to buy, and scarcely think of as investments, are safe, easy, reassuring, unexciting securities, like Canada Savings Bonds (CSBs) or guaranteed-investment certificates (GICs). A mother we know bought CSBs — not that they're always a bad choice, but she put most of her nest egg in one basket, one large, bland basket, because it seemed safe. And we know another widow whose advisor put her tiny inheritance (insurance money) into two GICs, which pay the woman her only income on a bi-monthly basis. At the time it seemed practical and safe, but a five-year GIC can be a drag in its third and fourth years if interest rates have gone up. And since you have to pay tax after the first $1,000 you earn on investments, it's not such a good idea. Still, a lot of widows buy them. We'll get to that. We'll get to all that.

Women are angry now. We've had enough of "Oh, don't you worry your pretty little head about that," because too many of us have had headaches after the fact — especially after the fact of divorce or widowhood. We're tired of being treated as mental incompetents. It's time we stopped feeling so dumb, stopped feeling so scared, stopped feeling angry. It's time we had a little fun, gained a little confidence and started looking after ourselves.

It Can Be Fun

To men, money is a game. If you don't believe us, watch any man play Monopoly. To most men, money is a tool to manipulate and a source of entertainment. Money is not something to be possessed.

10

Money, *per se*, is a success symbol, and so are the toys it buys. American feminist writer Victoria Billings has commented, "Whether he admits it or not, a man has been brought up to look at money as a sign of his virility, a symbol of his power, a bigger phallic symbol than a Porsche."

Women, on the other hand, according to writer Phyllis Chesler, are more ready to talk about orgasms than about money, probably because they understand their sexuality better than they understand finances. Not any more. We can all come out of the closet now and talk about money.

Who Am I?

Everyone asks herself this question sooner or later. In your case, it's probably later, but don't worry, it's not too late, and you're not alone in your wonder. Women of our generation, give or take a couple, have come of age later than is good for us. Women of our daughters' generation aren't that far ahead. One of our daughters just cashed in her RRSP to pay for her honeymoon. No comment; we're just telling you the facts.

In some times past, women never came of age at all. They were kept as pampered dolls or they were cast-off playthings. They seldom had any autonomy, and their knowledge of money was zilch, which didn't matter much because they never had any.

When Nora slammed the door in Ibsen's nineteenth-century play, *A Doll's House*, the sound was a slam that (slowly, slowly) was heard around the world. She was the doll in her husband's house, the perpetual child who, through trying to save her husband, enmeshed herself in a financial complication that ultimately opened her eyes to her own glass cage and silken bonds. We've all been like Nora, blind both to our own incompetence and our own eagerness to accept others' terms and definitions for our lives. No more.

Divorce, widowhood, delayed marriage, careers and renounced or curtailed motherhood have all been factors in reducing women's incompetence and ignorance in the world of finance. No one can afford to be helpless any more. Whether responsibility has been achieved, grabbed or thrust upon one, it has come about, accompanied by an eagerness to learn.

You see, you are no longer your father's daughter, your husband's wife (or ex-wife or widow), your child's mother or even your company's "girl." You are a person in your own right and you're going to stand on your own two feet, just as soon as you find and pay for a place to stand. With your name on it. "Money makes the man" goes the saying. It also makes the woman. Without money of her own, a woman scarcely has an identity these days.

"From birth to 18," said Sophie Tucker, "a girl needs good parents. From 18 to 35, she needs good looks. From 35 to 55, she needs a good personality. From 55 on, she needs good cash."

The Need for Cash

You need cash, especially if you're the single-parent head of a household (the fastest increasing sort of family unit in North America), female and poor. Oddly enough, if you have a full-time job, you probably have almost as good an income as that of a married woman living with her husband. It has been predicted that by the year 2000 all the poor in the United States will be women and their children. (What happens to men's children?) Never mind where the fathers are. They're not the ones who are feeding and clothing and educating those kids. That's considered to be the woman's job. And then she still has to have something to live on when she's through, when she hits the twilight zone and waits for darkness to descend. So cash is what she needs.

"Most women are only one man away from welfare" is the slogan of welfare-rights groups. It's going to take a while to change laws and status and pensions, let alone salaries, so that women have a chance for survival. In the meantime, there are ways a woman can help herself to a better future. That's what this book is for, to show you some of the ways, point a finger, pat you on the head, slap you on the back, lend a helping hand and count the ways.

Your Horizontal Profile

The first time one woman heard that expression she thought her advisor was getting fresh! A horizontal profile is just that, however: if you were dead and laid out flat tomorrow, what would you look like stretched out? How much would you be worth? It's stock-taking time. You don't have to die in order to take stock. Just stop dead in your tracks and look around. Who are you and how much are you worth?

Step One — Your Net Worth

Accountants use "assets" and "liabilities" to work out people's net-worth statements all the time. If that sounds a little too grand for you, remember that *assets* are what you own, *liabilities* are what you owe. Your net worth is what you own minus what you owe.

Doing a net-worth statement for you or your family may surprise you. You may not have much money in the bank but when you add up the value of what you do have — furniture, appliances, investments, a car, clothes, cash value of insurance and pension plans, jewellery, art and so on — you might be pleasantly surprised.

A net-worth statement tells you what you are worth today, right now. Tomorrow will be different because new bills will come in and others will be paid off. You should do a net-worth statement every six months or once a year so that you can see for yourself how well you are doing.

No two net-worth statements are alike. Don't worry if you can't fill in many of the blanks on our sample or if you have things we didn't think of listing. One woman wanted to know where her horse and pedigreed dog fit into a net-worth statement. Both are assets if they have a value and/or a selling price. Feed, stabling and vet charges are all liabilities.

If you have a year's supply of food in your freezer, don't forget to list the food, as well as the freezer, as an asset.

Most people use realistic selling prices *today* to put a value on their assets. Calls to your company pension office and your life-insurance agent will get you the cash values for pension and insurance; bank-books and up-to-date investment statements will help, as will last year's income-tax returns and recent selling prices for houses in your area. For some items, "guesstimates" will probably be the best you can do.

Liabilities are easier to calculate because debts are usually well documented. Some people like to do two net-worth statements — one with realistic selling prices on every item, the other using replacement values. It is useful to know how much it would cost, at today's prices, to replace everything one has, if only because it makes one more careful.

Take a blank sheet and label it "Net-Worth Statement," adding the date and marking one half "Assets" and the other half "Liabilities." Everything you own goes under the asset side. If you are doing the statement for yourself and you own half the house, put half the realistic selling price under assets; if half the mortgage is yours, that figure goes under liabilities.

Start off in pencil, with a large eraser close by. Expect to make mistakes. The first time you tackle such a statement it will take you a long time to get all the items listed and valued. Next time round it will be much easier.

13

Net-Worth Statement — Doe family, January ___, 198__

Assets		Liabilities	
Description:	*Value*	*Description:*	*Total Owing*
House/condo/mobile home		House mortgage	
Rental property		Other mortgage	
Lake cottage/ski chalet		Loans:	
Car		bank	
Boat		car	
Travel trailer		boat	
Sports equipment		personal	
Camping equipment		Credit-card balances:	
Household:		gas company	
furniture		retail stores	
appliances		bank card	
other goods		general card	
Antiques		Taxes payable:	
Silver (flatware)		income	
China		property	
Glassware		Insurance premiums payable:	
Art		property	
Books		life	
Stereo/TV		car	
Records/cassettes			
Camera(s)			
Binoculars			
Typewriter			
Home computer			
Home office equipment			
Gold/silver:			
coins			
certificates			
Clothing			
Furs			
Jewellery			
Bank accounts:			
savings			
chequing			
Bonds:			
Canada Savings			
others			

Assets		Liabilities	
Description:	Value	Description:	Total Owing
Stocks			
Mutual Funds			
GICs/term deposits			
Cash value:			
company pension			
life insurance			
RRSP			
RHOSP			
Collectibles:			
posters			
dolls			
china plates			
quilts			
stamps			
comics			
baseball cards			
others			
Prepaid taxes:			
income			
property			
Miscellaneous			
Totals:			

Net worth — assets minus liabilities. Work it out and see where you are.

Almost everyone who does a net-worth statement is pleased with the results. First of all, she actually did it, and second, she is worth more than she thought she was.

On the other hand, remember what multi-millionaire J. Paul Getty said: "If you can figure out how much you're worth, you aren't worth much." Well, maybe not in his terms, but it feels good to see it on paper. After doing a net-worth statement, no woman can ever again claim that she doesn't need to bother making a will because she has nothing to leave anyone.

How Much Do You Make A Year?

To know how to manage money, you first have to know what money there is to manage. It is amazing how few people have a clear idea of their actual annual incomes.

Teachers tell you how much they get for 10 months of the year; nurses and civil servants tend to refer to their twice-a-month paycheque totals; other workers often only know what they get per week. It is a rare woman who knows exactly what her gross (everything before deductions) salary totals or how much income comes into the household every year.

Let's find out how much money you have to cope with annually. That means another list. Include salary, regular bonuses or overtime, interest from bank accounts, income from Canada Savings Bonds, Guaranteed Investment Certificates or term deposits, dividends, even that $25 Aunt Edith has been sending every Christmas since heaven knows when. If you own rental property or receive alimony or maintenance payments, a pension or annuity cheque, add those in, too.

Making a list like this takes some remembering, references back to last year's income-tax return and up-to-date bank-books and investment statements. If you are doing it for your family, it will probably also take a lot of prodding and pleas for co-operation. If you can manage it, get the whole family involved. (Youngsters learn to manage money by watching their parents and other adults and noting their attitude to cash, bank accounts and investing. The best example of all is to get the kids to take part in the planning process. It might even do them some good to do an income sheet of their own, listing their allowances and interest that they earn on their bank accounts or on Canada Savings Bonds, if any.)

Some income, such as Canada Savings Bond interest, comes in only once a year; interest on GICs, term-deposits or bank accounts may be credited monthly, quarterly, semi-annually or annually; dividends are normally paid quarterly. If the money comes in on a basis other than monthly, figure out what the annual total is and put it in under the "annual" column. For monthly payments multiply by 12 to get the annual figure.

You can do a separate income sheet for each wage-earner if you are trying to work out family income, or you can put figures for both people in the "monthly" and "annual" columns to have all the information you need on one sheet.

Income:	Monthly	Annually
Wages/salary		
Regular bonuses		
Regular overtime		
Pension		
Annuity		
Rental income		
Maintenance		
Alimony		
Family Allowances		
Canada Savings Bond interest		
Other bond interest		
Bank interest		
Term deposit/GIC interest		
Dividends		
Regular gifts		
Miscellaneous		
Total		

Outgo

Where does all that money go? A lot of people have their fingers in your pie long before you get any money at all. Just take a quick look at the deductions listed on your salary slips and you will see what we mean. It is time for yet another list:

Deductions:	Monthly	Annual
Income tax		
Unemployment Insurance		
Canada Pension Plan		
Company pension plan		
Group insurance		
Medical/hospitalization/dental plan		
Union dues		
Parking		
Canada Savings Bonds payroll deductions		
Taxable added benefits		
Charities		
Others		
Totals:		

Please note that the Canada Pension Plan payments are not constant over the year; often the first payments in the year are much higher than expected and the total for the year is paid within a few months. That may mean that you don't pay any CPP toward the end of the year, having paid it all earlier. In this case it may be easiest to include the total under "annual" rather than to try to work it out on a monthly basis.

Now you have established your net worth. You know what comes in every year and what goes out before you see your paycheque. What is left is called "discretionary income" — what you have to shelter and feed you. It can be stretched so that you can save for some of the things you really want in life.

What Do You Really Want?

Psychology Today reported on a readership survey about money in the May 1981 issue. People answered detailed and intimate questions about their expenditures, aspirations and attitudes towards money. "How important is money?" was a key question. The answer was surprising to us. Finances were third in order of importance in people's minds, behind a love relationship and work. Here, in percentages, was the rating given to the most important aspects of life:

Love relationship	30
Work	19
Finances	15
Parenthood	14
Social life	13
Fun	9
Religion	8

(The above numbers are averages of percentages given by survey respondents. They, therefore, do not add up to exactly 100%.)

If you find that money is occupying a lot of your mind-time, you're not alone. Money may not buy happiness but it helps it along.

So stand up and prepare to count and be counted. You have work to do and a lot of living to do and fun to have before you're finished. Money talks, it is said, and it's time we started listening to it.

Money

"Money," wrote Gertrude Stein, "is really the difference between men and animals, most of the things men feel animals feel and vice versa, but animals do not know about money, money is purely a human conception and that is very important to know, very, very important.'' It's also important because up to now it has been purely a *male* conception. "Money is the man" goes a German proverb. Now money is about to become the woman, and very becoming it is, too.

2

Money Therapy

"I think I could be a good woman if I had five thousand [pounds] a year."
BECKY SHARP IN THACKERAY'S *VANITY FAIR*

How Much Money Does It Take?

The son of a friend of ours was about nine years old when he came home from school eager to write an assignment: "What I Want to Be When I Grow Up." But later he went to his mother in frustration when he couldn't find his vocation in the encyclopaedia under M for "Millionaire." Little girls, by that age, have their sights set on nursing or teaching or motherhood. Conditioning has already separated the boys from the girls. Not that there's anything wrong with service, but does it have to be penalized? Neither mothers nor nurses earn millions.

Remember Scarlett O'Hara (our favourite widow)? She used to have those terrible nightmares, and Rhett Butler would hold her and comfort her and ask her, "What is it you really want, Scarlett?" And she'd say, "I want enough money to be able to tell everybody to go to hell." The question is, how much money does it take?

For some people, not too much. You don't really want to consign other people to a hot place; you'd just like to come in out of the cold yourself. It's up to you to decide now what you really want. Know your priorities. One woman's luxury is another woman's necessity, and it's important to know the difference, to you. We knew a poor and struggling widow who didn't mind not having new clothes to wear, but who insisted on two things that kept up her morale and made her feel good about herself. One was her favourite French perfume; the

21

other was a Sassoon haircut. As long as her head looked good and she smelled nice, she was okay. Other women, though, in similar situations, prefer to buy a new dress or take music lessons. Whatever gets you through the hard parts.

Money Means . . .

Money means different things to different people. To a lot of people, it means status. It's a way of keeping score, of knowing that one counts. To others, money means security: a roof over one's head, food in the freezer, money in the bank. Still others need money to know who they are. The security they need is a sense of self.

Dr. Paul Lerner, a Toronto psychoanalyst, has described money as "psychic food." It's like mother's milk to some people — "not wealth guaranteed, but a return to the mother's breast." They never get enough. But misers, Lerner says, are "anally fixated"; they want to retain money, hoard it, hang onto it. Their desire to hold onto money is part of their desire to hold onto everything. You've heard of people who are "stinking" or "filthy" rich. That's why. To such a person, it isn't the money that's important; it's the acquiring of it, and the having it all to oneself, beyond need or usefulness. You don't see many misers these days. Thrift is a virtue that has fallen into disuse. As for turning everything into gold (not worth what it was a few years ago), King Midas would rather go berserk with a charge card.

Money is a mirror to the narcissist. Self-worth is measurable in dollars and cents. Narcissists like head waiters who call them by name and clothes with other peoples' names — like Yves St. Laurent or Gucci — all over them. That's how these people know they're special. That costs quite a lot.

Michael Godkewitsch is a senior consultant in employee-development research and services for Imperial Oil. He says, "Money is a very good substitute for feelings of inadequacy." Money can't buy happiness, but it can "create a sense of security and possibility." Or, as Joe E. Lewis put it, "Money may not be important but it quiets the nerves."

"Only when I am penniless do I believe that wealth brings unhappiness," said Canadian diarist Martin Roher. Lots of people feel that way; it's compensatory thinking. But it's not really thinking.

What Does Money Mean to You?

You have to learn to look at money without all these symbolic overtones. You have to know how *you* feel about it. You may have to look at your childhood. Some people felt so deprived in their youths that they'll never have enough money or be able to spend enough to make up for their real or imagined lack of money today. Other people (including our parents) never got over the Great Depression. They kept on being frugal long after it was over. But deprivation can trigger different responses in different people. Do you know yourself well enough to know how you respond?

You know that line, "You can never be too rich or too thin," attributed to the Duchess of Windsor, among others. But how rich is rich, let alone too rich? It's like age. Age is always 10 or 15 years older than you are. Similarly, rich is $10,000 or $15,000 more than you have. Such figures are dangerous. Economists have discovered that once a person/family is earning $20,000 a year, spending habits escalate to $10,000 a year more than that. And that is the beginning of poverty. Poverty isn't being broke; poverty is never having enough.

"Money," says Michael Godkewitsch, "is not the end-all of compensation. But it's the begin-all."

So begin by analyzing how much money you want and what you want it for.

Examine Your Goals

How many of your goals are really yours and how many of them have been implanted by the society you live in? How many of them are hangovers from pipe dreams you had when you were a child and how many are still valid? How many of them are other people's values or hopes for you and how many of them are genuinely yours? How many of them are related to your life and how many of them are irresponsible fantasies?

You know the story of the man who put a tall ladder up against the wall of a house and climbed and climbed and climbed, in such a hurry to get to the top that he didn't discover till he got there that he'd put the ladder against the wrong house? Sometimes we do that with our goals, set our sights on something that's wrong for us, that isn't what we really want. Don't wait until it's too late to discover that what you thought you wanted from life isn't that at all. You'll save yourself a lot of time and effort if you define your goals accurately.

Where Do You Want to Be?

Where do you want to be, what do you want to have — in one month? Five months? Five years? Write it all down under three columns for immediate, short-term and long-term goals. And if you want, you can

23

add a fourth column, for the twilight zone — retirement. You can be very general, and write down security, health, love or companionship, work, travel. Or you can write very specific desires: a new coat, a new car, to get out of debt, save the down payment for a house, get a college education for you or your children, have Mary's teeth straightened. Go ahead and put everything down, including your fantasies. You can sort out your priorities later. This is how you discover them.

If you've put down only things — that is, material goods and luxuries — in your list of goals, take a few more minutes and write down activities you'd like to experience. Then take another few minutes and describe the person you'd like to be: thinner? more patient? calmer? Sometimes those qualities cost money as well. It's hard to be thinner if you're living on cheap pasta and bread. It's hard to be patient if you're crammed into a few rooms with your children and no one ever has any privacy. It's hard to be calm if you're eaten up with anxiety about how to pay the heating bill and where you're going to get the money to buy new shoes for the kids.

Human Needs

Psychologist Abraham Maslow, who made us all want to be self-fulfilling personalities, cited a hierarchy of needs for the human being. Basic are the needs for survival (food, shelter, safety), and then come the needs for personal development and growth. Once our basic needs have been met, they no longer motivate us. "Grub first, then ethics," as Bertolt Brecht put it. The best things in life, goes the song, are free. The trick is to reach that point. Sometimes it costs a lot to get there.

All legitimate goals cost time and effort and money. See them clearly, for what they mean to you and what they may cost. Then sort them out, in order of priority.

Make a List

If your list reads:
- $1,000 in a savings account within the next year
- pay off credit card debts of $480 within six months
- $2,000 for a smashing holiday three years from now

you have something to shoot for. You can plan.

Saving that $1,000 in the next year will cost you about $83 a month ($83 x 12 = $996 and with interest you will be well over the mark); paying off those credit cards will cost you $80 per month ($480 divided

24

by six); saving for your holiday will mean a monthly commitment over three years of about $55 ($2,000 divided by 36 = $55.55).

Any or all of these goals may be achievable. What it is going to take to reach them is planning, budgeting and perhaps some scrimping.

Once you've decided what you want, ask yourself:

- are my goals realistic?
- am I willing to give up what it would take to achieve them (for example, $55 a month for three years for that special holiday)?
- am I willing to compromise to achieve what I want?
- will my plan affect my family, and if so, what am I prepared to do about it?

The next question is: "How can I handle my present income to save the amount I want?" Some goal-oriented people vow not to take any "new" money into normal income. If they get a raise or a bonus, or an unexpected cash gift, they pretend they never got the money and stash it away in a "special-goals" account. If you are expecting a six-per-cent raise this year, five-per-cent next, take those increases and put them into your special account for something you really want. It's not hard to do once you have made up your mind on a specific goal and have committed yourself to achieving it.

Make sure you set some benchmarks along the way so that you can check on how you are doing. If you don't reach the benchmarks successfully, change them; if you stumble, try again. When your first goal is in sight, set up a new one.

A Woman's Reach

Just make sure your goals are within reach. In your lifetime, that is. Some people have managed to achieve the impossible dream, like a huge, gorgeous house, but it took them so long to get it that they had little time or life left to enjoy it. Consider the cost of your goals, not only in terms of money, but in terms of time, effort, life and sacrifice.

If you're married, you might find it worthwhile to work out these goals with your spouse. Then you'll know whether you both want the same things and you can decide how to work together to achieve them. It's just as well to be agreed before you start. A couple may say that they want to save the down payment for a house, but if one of them keeps suggesting dinner out in an expensive restaurant once or twice a week, such extravagance may sabotage the stated goal of the two of them.

If you have a basic disagreement, then perhaps you can work out a compromise and save for something you both want. Or, if both of you work, then one of you can save for the trip you've always wanted to take and the other one can save for a new car. Compromise is a viable form of negotiation. No marriage, as no contract, should be without it.

Yours, Mine and Ours

While we're on the subject of couples, this is a good point at which to stop, if you haven't already, and figure out exactly who pays for what. The dual-income family is a fact of life now, but how couples spread their dual incomes around varies greatly from family to family. In some households, the man pays for the necessities (that is, shelter and food) and the woman buys the holidays and entertainment. Unless they have a marriage contract, this can be awkward (see page 147). Other couples take a what's-mine-is-yours attitude to everything and pool their resources in a joint account, from which they pay all their expenses. This, too, has its pitfalls. Neither one has any discretionary money, any money of his or her own. Though joint accounts speak of wonderful trust and sharing, we do recommend separate accounts as well.

"Yours, mine and ours" is a livable motto, but it takes some working out and is subject to highly individual solutions. It's especially difficult, but probably most important to solve, in the case of the stay-at-home homemaker with no income of her own. We know a young man who from his earliest days of marriage paid his wife a wage for her home-making activities, a set percentage of his income. This money went into her own account without strings; it was to be used at her discretion. On the other hand, we know a man who refused to take out any kind of insurance on the life of his wife, mother of his young children, because, he said, she wouldn't cost much to replace. Inevitably, when we start talking about money, we end up with human relationships!

All we can say is, keep the doors of communication open, but keep some money for yourself. Money talks, too.

Where Are You Going?

Now we'll get to the really hard questions. Where would you like to be when you are 65 or so? We are very concerned about aging single women. There are so many of them. And they're poor. "Women living alone are five times more vulnerable to poverty," according to the Welfare Council's report. So while you were writing down your goals in life, we hope you gave a thought to the old lady in your future. She's up there waiting for you and what you do for her now is going to affect her/your life directly in the not-so-distant future. Give the old lady a long, long thought when you come to the chapter on retirement and do some thoughtful planning that will make life better for both of you by the time you join her.

You may think that because you're married now, that lonely old lady isn't waiting for you. Sorry, but think again. Take a look at the table on life patterns of Canadian women, taken from the Welfare Council's report. Seventy-four out of a hundred women will end up having to look after themselves.

Every married woman is a potential widow or divorcée these days. So every woman owes herself basic money competence; she *must* know how to take care of herself. It's called independence and it's not an unattractive quality. It's also a saving one.

Constance Dowling, in her book, *The Cinderella Complex*, maintains that deep inside every woman lurks this need to be dependent, to have someone take care of her. People who live in glass shoes shouldn't kick thrones, but you and we know better. We don't need a fairy godmother to get us out of this mess, or a Prince Charming. We just want the magic wand — money.

Life Patterns of Canadian Women

Age

Adolescence

*Age 18
to 50*

*Age 50
and older*

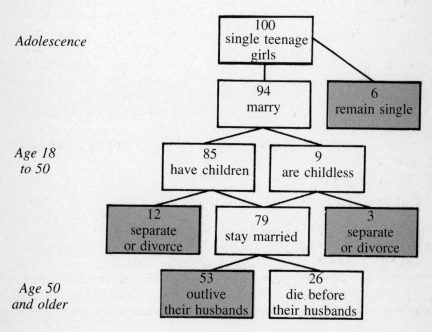

Whether you're rich or poor, it's always nice to have money. We women have had so little opportunity to have it, we tend to think poor. So we have to do a little prosperity training. It's hard for a woman to realize, when she has been trying to keep warm by rubbing nickels and dimes together, that if she learns to spend money creatively it will come back to her, that she needn't follow the careful, often fearful, spending habits of her parents, that she can give herself permission to be affluent. Or if not affluent, at least solvent. It's inconvenient to be poor, an inconvenience we can live without. So we're going to change our feelings and attitudes to money and, along the way, our feelings and attitudes about ourselves.

> Certainly there are lots of things in life that money won't buy,
> but it's very funny —
> Have you ever tried to buy them without money?

Ogden Nash said that. Now, what do *you* say? What are you: a victim, a product or mistress of your fate?

3

Women and Credit

"Money is a poor man's credit card."
MARSHALL McLUHAN

You Do Not Exist

The strange fact is that in these parlous times, if you don't owe or have never owed any money then you do not exist. You do not own a credit rating until you have owed and paid back money. A credit rating is not only the reputation but the record of your previous ability to pay back money you have borrowed.

Paper and noisy money is for transit systems and parking lots and take-out coffee. Plastic credit is for identification (when you want to cash a cheque they'd rather look at your credit card than your bank account); for buying a car, or for coping with an emergency (the freezer that just died at the beginning of a long weekend). Without credit you wouldn't be able to borrow enough money to do these things because no one would have ever heard of you. By no one, we mean a credit manager or banker. (For that matter do you know him/her? You should, and he/she should know your name. Go and introduce yourself to-morrow. That's for starters.)

Earning a Credit Rating

The fastest way to earn a credit rating is to borrow money (we'll get to that) and pay it back promptly. If your bank doesn't report to a credit bureau, you can. You have proof that you pay your debts. You have a history. You now exist, on paper.

There are other ways to go down in credit history. Open chequing

29

and savings accounts in your own name, if you haven't already done so. (You can do that while you're learning your bank manager's name.) While you're there, apply for a credit card and for a limit, that is, the maximum amount of money you are allowed to charge on your credit card. If you use the card well, that is, if you pay your bill regularly, promptly, and in full, you can soon apply to raise your limit because you'll have a good track record. Get a utility or your phone account in your name and pay the bills regularly, too.

Next, open a charge account in your name at a retail store. Again, pay your bill as soon as you receive it. You want to impress all those credit managers with your sterling character. Besides, the interest on credit is terrible and a total waste of your money. If the larger retail stores say you don't qualify, try to get a card from one of the smaller ones. Buy only things you need, pay the bills on time and create a credit history for yourself. With a good reputation, it should be easy to get a card from a major retailer.

If you're single and already have credit cards, be sure to keep them in your name when and if you get married. You have to be an independent economic entity. If you're married and have a Mrs. card, as in *Mrs. John Doe*, apply to the bank, store or gas company for a card reading *Mrs.* (or *Ms.*?) *Jane Doe* and ask for a separate file in your name. Then go and borrow some money and pay it back.

Credit Bureaus

There are about 160 credit bureaus scattered across Canada, acting as clearing houses for credit-history information. In most cases, credit grantors such as banks, retail stores and utility companies pay fees to the local bureau, which keeps files on local residents who apply for or have credit. The grantors who belong to the bureau feed information to it and for a fee can get details from your files on where and when you have been granted credit and whether you have paid your bills on time.

Some credit bureaus count monthly payments for telephone, hydro and heating fuel as part of your credit history; others concentrate on your retail-store transactions.

If you have had financial trouble or been slow paying a bill or if you have disputed charges and refused to pay, the details will probably be in your file. So will information considered to be in the public domain, such as bankruptcies or judgments against you. All negative information has to be removed from your file after seven years, although writs are taken out, except in special circumstances, after one

30

year. (A writ is a formal order issued by a court directing the person[s] to whom it is addressed to do or refrain from doing some specific act.) Credit bureaus do not "rate" anyone's credit, but they do "provide a factual report on a consumer's credit history."

Credit bureaus' public relations people say that the staff is happy to have consumers drop in. (How happy?) They can't keep track of marriages and divorces and are pleased to bring files up to date.

You are also legally entitled to go through your file and check it for errors. It may not be your credit history at all. People who have been refused credit have sometimes found that they have been confused with someone else of the same name who has had a bad record.

You have the right to include information in your file that may correct what you consider to be errors or omissions. You can also include your side of an altercation if a credit grantor has sent in his.

In Victoria, the local credit bureau states in a brochure that if all your cards are in your husband's name you can ask to have a file opened for you. It will include information on your personal accounts and accounts in your husband's name that you use or where you are liable for payment. The brochure goes on to say in capital letters, "It is important for you to contact all of these credit grantors directly and request that they report the account history in both your name and your husband's." It explains further that unless you do this, your new file won't be updated because the information won't be submitted in both names.

It's a good idea, but one woman spent 16 hours trying to accomplish this. The major retailers and the local credit-bureau manager all admitted they didn't know how to do what the pamphlet said should be done. And the manager went so far as to ask her why she wanted credit anyway!

Provincial legislation controls the availability of credit reports. It is against the law for any credit bureau to give out information improperly or for anyone to ask for credit information under false pretenses. Usually, such information is only given out in relation to the extension of credit or insurance, a job application, a potential financial deal or the issuance of a special licence.

The Three Cs of Credit

Stores and companies and banks are looking for the Three Cs of Credit when they ask you to fill out their forms and answer their questions. These are Capacity, Character and Collateral.

Capacity

Capacity is simply the means to repay. You will be asked to give the name of the company you work for, the length of time you have been there, and how much money you owe.

Character

Character has nothing to do with your sexual habits or how you relate to your mother. Character is an assessment of your stability, account- ability and ability to pay bills on time. You'll be asked if you own or rent your home and how long you have lived there. You will be asked for other creditors' names. These will be checked out to see if you paid promptly. You will also be checked out to determine whether you have already borrowed more than you can possibly repay.

If for any reason you think you have been discriminated against and barred from access to credit because of your sex, do something about it. Even though the banks and major companies have laid down guide- lines on women's access to credit, it sometimes takes a while for this broader view to sift down to individual credit managers. If you think you're being given a hard time solely because of your sex (and not because you already owe $6,000 that you can't possibly repay), then act on your suspicion. Ask to see the senior credit officer and state your case, without hysterics or bitterness.

If you can't get any satisfaction there, try the Ministry of Consumer Relations, or whatever it's called in your province. The ministries are beginning to be sensitive to women's needs. Don't let the matter go unheeded. Every protest registered will make it easier for the next woman applying for credit.

Creditors can ask you how many dependants you have and how many other debts you have. Beyond that, in the realm of the personal, they should not go. There are still prejudices flying around, and you should be alert to them. If you're single, the theory is that you'll get married or move or both and leave your debts behind you. If you're married, you'll get pregnant and welsh on your payments. If you're separated, your support payments may stop, and then how will you pay your bills? If you're divorced, well, divorced women are unstable anyway, aren't they? As for widows, their income has stopped per- manently so they're not a good risk. We're not making this up. These are some of the prejudices you have to fight. In a ladylike but assertive way, of course.

Collateral is short for collateral security — some form of property or money you offer as security, in addition to your personal obligation. In case of sudden illness or unemployment, what other means do you have of repaying your debt? You will be asked if you own any property, such as your own home, or stocks or bonds, and whether or not you have a savings account. Sometimes creditors smile on women of property. Sometimes not. We know several women who free-lance in their fields and each of them reports frowns from creditors when they learn of this maverick way of earning a living. Essentially, they see you as unemployed. And a woman as well. Obviously a poor risk. One woman had to get her husband's signature. Another, divorced, referred the creditor to her accountant. As Gail Sheehy, author of *Passages*, put it, "The best way to attract money (is) to give the appearance of having it." And then there's John's Collateral Corollary: "In order to get a loan you must first prove you don't need it."

Care and Feeding of Credit Cards

Once you have your precious credit card, treat it as such. It is precious, and so is your credit rating. Don't go overboard, ever, with charge or credit cards. There is a difference, by the way. A *charge card*, such as American Express or Carte Blanche, is a card that allows you to run up a bill to an agreed limit. The bill must be paid in full upon receipt. A *credit card* (like Visa or Mastercard) is issued by your bank and gives you a line of credit through your bank. A line of credit is like a loan. The bill need not be paid in full at the end of each month, but beware of the interest charges. At the end of every spree is the reckoning and sometimes you wish the reckoning were dead — it or you.

If you know when your billing date is (it is usually about five days before the day you receive your statement), you can arrange to make your purchases just after the closing of the account for the previous month. Thus, you will not be billed for your new purchases until the next closing, and that bill will not be payable until three to four weeks later. For example, if your billing date is March 28, anything you charge after that will not appear on your bill until April, and you will not have to pay for it until three to four weeks later. You are using the bank's money, and also have the use of yours (which is bearing interest in a daily-interest savings account) until you pay the bill. This is called a float, and it's nice.

The trick is to keep all your money in a daily-interest savings (DIS) account, transferring funds to your chequing account only as you need them. But plan ahead because some DIS accounts now charge a fee for more than two withdrawals per month — they've all got you, coming and going!

A service charge is now being imposed on most credit cards, but you can still use your float. Just make sure you're getting more in interest than the service charge is costing you. If you charge $200 a month or more, you probably are.

Some people are experimenting with paying for everything by cheque or by cash, and you may want to investigate that line of action. But do you really want to carry that much cash all the time? And do you know what stores usually ask for in the way of identification when you want to cash a cheque? Besides your driver's licence, they'll ask to see a major credit card. And if you don't have an unlimited-cheque service in the banking plan you use, then you're paying for every cheque you write.

Perhaps compromise is the best solution. Cut down on the number of credit cards you own (after all the trouble you went through to get them); think twice before writing a cheque; keep on carrying less cash.

Use credit wisely, even creatively, and you will come out ahead. Let it get ahead of you and it may take months or even years to recover.

The Dangers of Plastic Money

We know a young woman who is a self-confessed credit-cardaholic. She can't walk through a department store with a credit card in her purse without buying something. To wean her from her cards, it was suggested she cut them all up. She did but then found the same trouble with her cheque book. At that point she said she had to find a bigger apartment because it was so crammed with things she neither wanted nor used, but was too embarrassed to return. The final solution was to persuade her to join her local Y. She signed up for lunch-hour exercises to keep her out of the stores. At last report she was buying less and exercising more but she had great plans for a shopping blow-out once her exercises resulted in a new shape!

Limits — Yours and Theirs

If you trust yourself, ask for your credit limit to be raised after you've proved you pay your bill regularly. You think you may not need it, but sometimes you do. A friend of ours was going on an extended business trip in Europe and knew she would need to use her Visa card

34

more than usual. It was mid-month when she left and she didn't feel like paying off her current bill until it was due. So before she left, she phoned to find out what her bill to date was and asked for her limit to be raised because of the trip. Request granted. But if a higher limit is merely added incentive for you to spend more money, don't ask for it.

Yes, we love our Visa cards. But we also love our American Express cards and we charge all our travel to them because Amex gives us travel insurance at a minimal extra cost. It is also useful for getting money in strange places at odd times. If you travel, as they say, don't leave home without it.

But that's an insidious slogan, and quite dangerous. We recommend that for short jaunts you do leave home without your credit and charge cards. Lock them away in a safe place and go without. Try it one week out of each month for starters. Impulse buying really does slow down when you don't have your instant credit with you, and you carry very little cash.

Credit Card Protection

Before you lock away your credit cards, tape them lightly to a sheet of paper and have them photocopied. Then file the copy of your cards, with those precious numbers, in a safe place. If they are ever stolen or lost, you have a complete record of the numbers. Report the loss immediately to the companies and they will stop the use of the cards. Be sure to keep the record up to date. Photocopy new cards as they are issued. You can also buy credit-card insurance, for a nominal cost, to protect you from some thief's mad orgy of spending on your cards, name and credit. Check with your general insurance agent about this. Who steals my purse steals trash, but who steals my credit card is getting away with a potential fortune.

Here are some other thoughts about credit cards and the ways you can protect yourself from scams with them:

Put a special, very noticeable mark on each card — a red star, a blue balloon, a green X — anything that you can quickly see. This helps to eliminate card-switching. Few people actually check to make sure they get back their own card in a restaurant or store; the mark makes identification easy and may stop a clerk from taking your card for payment and giving you back someone else's. If your card is switched, the person making the changeover has your card and a copy of your signature on his/her copy of your receipt and can have a real spree, courtesy of your carelessness.

35

It's important not only to hang onto your copy of a credit card receipt but also to tear up the carbon. Again, the number and signature/name are clearly shown and could lead to orders made in your name and with your number.

When you use your card, make sure you get, and keep, your receipt so you can check it against your monthly bill. If you throw it away, anyone picking it up has your name and number and can order merchandise by phone and you won't know what's happening until your bill comes at the end of the month.

Gas Card Swindles

If you pay for your gas by card, it is possible for an attendant to imprint a few extra blanks which he can fill out at his leisure. Be suspicious if your monthly bills look larger than usual or if you have several charges from stations you don't often use. Watch, too, that totals don't get changed. If you bought $3 worth of gasoline you don't want to be charged for $8 or even $13 worth!

As always, check your bills carefully and if there are discrepancies, report them immediately.

Credit Card Society

If you don't already, you will soon come to regard our easy-credit society with mixed feelings. On the one hand, it's nice to feel solvent most of the time, to be able to pay for an unexpected bargain at a sale or indulge in a spur-of-the-moment Japanese dinner. On the other hand, some bargains can be white elephants, difficult to care and pay for, and you don't want to pay interest on sukiyaki for four months. So be careful.

Happiness is knowing you can pay your charge bill in full at the end of each month. You won't even mind if your knight on a white charger never comes. You have your own charge card and it's in your name.

4
Banking

"Think of tomorrow,
Divide your pay in two,
Take what you need to live,
Put the balance in safety."
ANONYMOUS BANK PAY ENVELOPE MESSAGE, 1935

Banks provide more than storehouses for your money or bookkeeping services to keep track of it. Before a woman finds, needs, or can afford an accountant or stockbroker, she should take every advantage of the facilities a bank offers. There are twelve different types of accounts available now, each with its accompanying advantages (interest, service) and disadvantages (hidden costs). As with everything else, you should shop around, ask questions and compare.

Types of Accounts

Basically, there are four types of accounts: high-interest or premium-savings, daily-interest, daily-interest with chequing privileges, and personal chequing. As might be expected, the premium savings gives you the highest interest rate, but there's a catch. Although the interest is computed for each month, it is based on the lowest amount of money that was in the account during that month. Thus, if you fail to make a deposit until the second of the month, or if you have to withdraw money before the end of the month, you will receive interest only on the lowest sum, before deposit and after withdrawal. There are no chequing privileges.

Daily-interest savings accounts, although they earn less interest, are more flexible and respond immediately to a deposit by taking it into account for the month's reckoning. The catch here is that most banks allow only two withdrawals without charge. If you don't plan ahead

— that is, if you don't transfer enough funds to your chequing account to cover your expenses and have to go back to the well — you'll be charged a service charge. We don't like paying service charges when we don't have to.

Daily-interest chequing accounts eliminate this problem. The interest is lower, usually, but there is no charge for chequing if you keep a minimum stated balance in the account at all times (difficult sometimes). The monthly statement of this type of account serves as a kind of money manager, showing you exactly where your money has gone. The catch to this one is that you don't get your cancelled cheques back. If you should need a cheque to prove payment, the bank will search for it — for a fee, and only for a limited time period.

The personal-chequing account yields no interest at all but offers other services: usually a discount on your safety deposit box, no charges on utility payments and others made through the bank (a saving on postage), no charges on travellers' cheques, and some form of overdraft protection. Your cancelled cheques are returned to you with each month's statement. We find many of these little proofs of payment useful to us at income-tax time. They are also incontestable proof to stupid companies who insist you haven't paid them. You can make faces at them and cite the cheque number and date of the cheque they cashed. Don't, for heaven's sake, send them the cheque! If you need to send proof, photocopy the cheque and keep the original. Even if you trust the company, don't trust the mail.

Shop Around

As competition increases and banks, credit unions and trust companies offer more and more of the same services, it pays to look around and find out what accounts would serve you best.

Few of us realize what banks, trust companies and credit unions offer these days or how much they charge for their services. When was the last time you asked about the kinds of account you could have or the cost of writing a cheque or the meaning of a specific service charge?

After you have inquired about different accounts, interest rates, balance requirements, compounding and service charges, you can decide what accounts you need for what purposes. Be sure to take the location of the bank into consideration. (Can you walk there? Is there good parking? Is it on your usual circuit?) Then make a final decision on what accounts you should have where.

You may have been using a chequing/savings account when two

separate accounts would serve you better; there may be money sitting in a low-interest account that should be in a high-daily-interest one; your daily-interest account may pay only on a minimum monthly balance or compound semi-annually when what you really need is one that pays every day from the day you put money in until the day it comes out and compounds monthly. Keep asking questions till you find what you want.

Daily Interest That Isn't

Some people mistakenly think that if a bank has their money from the first of the month until 5:30 P.M. on the last day of the month that they have earned a month's interest. Not so. If the money is withdrawn from a minimum-monthly-balance account before the bank closes on the last day of the month, you won't get any interest on the amount withdrawn for the 30 or 31 days it was there. Be sure to check your account and see what's happening to your money.

Charges

If there are service charges on your monthly statement, find out what they are for and ask, too, for a list of standard charges. Don't be surprised if it takes several requests to get such a list. Some bank employees have even been known to tell customers that it is illegal to issue one!

Last summer, one of us noticed a six-dollar service charge that wasn't identified. When asked, the credit union concerned said it covered the cost of certifying a post-dated cheque that had been put through ahead of time. The cheque had been returned to the company that had submitted it, the firm then sent it back, asking for certification. This was done and the customer, the innocent party in all this, was charged!

Complaints to the teller and the local branch manager did no good, but a vice-president was horrified, admitted the practice was illegal and had the six dollars back in the account within hours. If the complaint hadn't gone higher we would still be short the six dollars and the branch probably would still be charging people illegally.

Another Horror Story

In British Columbia last year, a small-town bank made front-page news because a client complained about being charged different amounts for the same service within a short period of time. The bank clerk explained that she had been told she could charge what she thought the client would pay and that the money over and above the normal

39

charge could go into the branch's party fund! Naturally, the bank concerned said loudly and firmly that such action was not bank policy, but several other branches 'fessed up and said such charging had become a practice for them.

Banks Can Be Wrong

Many of us were brought up to believe that banks can do no wrong. We tend to take our bank statements as gospel and not question anything on them. A recent Consumers' Association of Canada survey showed that many of the respondents had found errors on their bank statements, not just once, but several times.

Legally, the banks are not responsible for mistakes shown on your statement if *you* don't catch the errors within a certain length of time. When your statement comes in, set aside some time that day to go through it thoroughly, matching deposits, withdrawals and cheques with your own records and cheque-book. Call immediately about any discrepancies and don't give up until you have the answers and the corrections.

People Can Be Wrong, Too

Quite recently, not far enough back in time to enable us not to blush to tell, one of us neglected to enter a cheque in her record book — more than once, in fact. That really messes up a balance. Remember always to add in the difference on a cheque you have marked "U.S. funds." (The exchange rate charged is shocking; send a U.S. money order.) Some magazines, as you know, require payment in American money; when you don't know what the exchange is, you write "U.S. funds." When that cheque clears, be sure to deduct the extra amount to keep your balance accurate. Something else one of us forgets to do is to take off the monthly charge for the personal service plan or key account or whatever your bank calls such special service. This same klutz also has a monthly premium on an insurance policy that is deducted automatically and guess who forgets to enter this withdrawal half the time?

It's little things like that that throw you off balance. Check them all before you accuse the bank of making an error.

How to Balance Your Cheque-Book

As to making your cheque-book agree with your bank statement, here's how: put your cancelled cheques in order, by date and number. If you don't get cancelled cheques back, you'll have to use your statement and your record book. Now go through the cheques one by one, but stop after every three. Add up the amounts and subtract that amount from the balance that was in your cheque-book before you wrote those three cheques. If you're lucky, and good at arithmetic, you should get the same number as the new balance in your cheque-book. Lots of luck!

Remember Stephen Leacock's funny essay "My Financial Career"? The poor man got rattled inside a bank. A lot of people do, including one of us. (We won't tell you which one.)

Banking Pitfalls

In her excellent book, *Don't Bank On It*, Alix Grainger goes through the banking process step by step. She cites numerous examples of how consumers can get caught when they don't watch out for themselves.

In many instances it's a case of buyer beware. People often sign up for monthly package deals with banks, not completely understanding either what the packages cost or what they offer.

One thing promised by some package accounts is overdraft protection, which allows you to overdraw your account and not be charged for the overdraft. Instead, the bank charges the amount to your bank card. Even if the overdraft is only $10 and is covered by you within 24 hours, you will be charged interest on your Visa or Mastercard for a minimum cash withdrawal of $50 for 30 days. You can avoid this by instructing your bank in writing to withdraw the amount required to cover the cheque from your savings account. That way you don't pay interest.

An Agreement Between You and The Bank

Many people don't realize that when they fill out a card opening an account they are actually signing an agreement with the bank. Make sure you read all the fine print (sometimes you need a magnifying glass to do that) and understand what it means.

Usually banks insist that it is your responsibility to make sure that your accounts are in good order. When you sign the application form for an account, you may be agreeing that in case of any dispute the bank can debit your account.

Don't be surprised to find that the bank has debited your account:

- when it writes to you to say you haven't used your account recently;
- if you don't pay the minimum balance on your charge card

41

issued by the bank (in this case you can eliminate the problem if you keep your bank accounts in a bank other than the one which issued you the card);

- if your husband overdraws the family's joint account and doesn't have a separate account in his own name at that bank, but you do;
- if there is a discrepancy between what you say you deposited through a banking machine and what the bank says you have deposited. In fact, be careful about depositing any money in the machines because the card you get back is not considered to be a legal receipt. The application form you fill out for a banking machine card does spell this out, but few customers really understand it.

Next-Day Banking

Consumers are often upset when they go into their banks after lunch and find every teller has a sign proclaiming that all the transactions are for the next business day's date. Bank officials tell us that, regardless of the sign, if you deposit money on a Friday the deposit is credited to your account on that day. And, of course, if you take money out of your account, the withdrawal is also debited as of that day.

But just to be sure, tell your teller that you want that day's date on your transaction. Then check to make sure it is recorded in your passbook or on any receipt you get. If the teller refuses, ask to speak to the manager and carry your complaint to the district supervisor or even to the Canadian Bankers' Association if you have to.

The Canada Deposit Insurance Corporation (CDIC)

As of early April 1983, and retroactive to January, the CDIC insures deposits in each bank up to a total of $60,000. That figure would cover RRSPs, an RHOSP, chequing/savings and savings accounts in all branches of the one bank. Therefore, if you have $65,000 worth of such assets in a Royal Bank of Canada branch or branches, you might consider moving $5,000 to another bank (not just another branch) in order to qualify for the coverage.

Few people realize there is a five-year limit to coverage by the CDIC. That means a five-year term deposit or Guaranteed Investment Certificate would be covered; one sold for any period more than five years would not be.

All federally incorporated trust companies are also covered by the CDIC but those chartered provincially may not necessarily be members and coverage may be different. Find out about yours.

Credit unions have their own kind of insurance coverage for money left with them.

The CDIC puts out a small booklet in both official languages spelling out the details of its coverage and explaining, for example, that joint accounts are insured separately, that both interest and capital are protected, that contents of safety-deposit boxes are not insured and that if a member institution ceases to be insured, it is up to that institution to notify its depositors. For your copy write to:

Canada Deposit Insurance Corporation,
P.O. Box 2340, Station D,
Ottawa, Ontario   K1P 5W5

Safety-Deposit Boxes

Not only are safety-deposit boxes not insured under the CDIC, but banks take no direct responsibility for your box or its contents. After all, if the box or its contents are lost, stolen or destroyed, how can you prove what was there?

Jewellery, gems, silver and gold bullion should be insured separately or under a floater policy; lost stock certificates can be replaced, as can bonds. However, it is up to you to know exactly what is in your safety-deposit box at all times and to make your own arrangements for insuring it.

In order to get restitution from a bank, you would have to prove that you had what you said you had in a box, that the bank was negligent and that the contents were actually gone. All of this is almost impossible to prove to a court's satisfaction.

All banks do take responsibility for normal precautions. But if someone breaks through a wall into a bank vault and your box is burglarized, unless you have insured its contents yourself, you are out of luck.

Automatic Tellers

Electronic banking is alive and well in Canada. Consumers are now able to use bank cards and machines to transfer money from one account or branch to another, to pay bills, to make deposits and withdrawals or to take cash advances on their Visa or Mastercard cards.

Getting an electronic bank card is simple — there are no age restrictions, no minimum bank balances required. All you need is an account in the bank from which you want the card. This type of banking simplifies your life considerably if you are travelling and run out of money or if you wish to bank at odd hours. Most machines across Canada are accessible 24 hours a day.

Before you get a card, check what it will allow you to do and what it will cost. Some banks allow you to pay utility bills at no charge, one charges 60¢ per bill. Another's card is good for withdrawals only.

The key to electronic banking is your personal identification number (PIN), which activates the machine in your name. Either you or your bank choose your number. Never, under any circumstances, reveal it to anyone, even a banking official, unless you want it to be used by someone else.

For all these conveniences, automatic tellers should be used with care. Think twice before depositing cash through an automatic teller. You have no proof of the amount deposited, should a discrepancy appear in your statement. And remember that cash advances charged to your Visa or Mastercard account result in immediate interest charges at the current rate of interest. Consumers usually expect the advances to be treated as ordinary Visa or Mastercard expenditures with no interest applied until the next billing date.

Winnipeg, the city in which we both grew up, had a motto over the arched doorway of the city hall. "Commerce, Prudence, Industry" were the watchwords of our home town, no doubt inspired by the same Scots who made curling such a tradition in Manitoba. We keep thinking of those qualities as we write this book. They should be part of every woman's arsenal. Prudence, we would venture to say, has to do with banking. Sock it away for another day.

5

Borrowing

"If you'd know the value of money go and borrow some."
BENJAMIN FRANKLIN

"Live within your income, even if you have to borrow to do so."
JOSH BILLINGS

"But of all evils, to borrow money is perhaps the worst."
SUSANNA MOODIE

"I have never been afraid to borrow."
E.P. TAYLOR

Forgive us for such a mosaic of quotations, but there you have the ambivalence of attitudes toward borrowing, and the nervousness that women feel about it. Women have been much more apprehensive about borrowing money than men. They don't want to be in anyone's debt. They want to be responsible citizens, so they cling to old Polonius's advice ("Neither a borrower nor a lender be"). These days, you can't afford *not* to be a borrower. But be a creative one.

Borrowing

Much of what we've said about getting credit applies to borrowing money, because credit isn't really *credit*, it's a loan. If you need some money for a new car, a holiday, a pet project (a computer?) or just to establish your own credit rating, then go ahead and borrow money. Banks, trust companies and credit unions are more willing to lend money to women these days than they were a few years ago, though there are still some obstacles to borrowing.

The institutions are all much more likely to want to lend money to you if you have a good, steady job with a fairly large income, own your own car and home and have a sizable net worth. But if you were in that position, you probably wouldn't need a loan.

Getting a Loan

Before you make that trip to the bank or credit union, figure out how much you could afford to devote to loan payments from your present paycheque. Give yourself some leeway in case of emergency, knowing that if no emergency pops up you can always put the extra money on the loan.

Find out exactly what amount you need to borrow and be prepared to defend your need. If you have never tried to borrow money before, write out a short script detailing what you need the loan for and how much you think would be adequate. Practise in front of your mirror until you are comfortable with the request and then arm yourself for battle with:

- an up-to-date net-worth statement, which you can leave with a loans officer, showing exactly what you own and what you owe;
- details of any previous loans you have paid back on time;
- a list of any outstanding debts you have at the moment;
- a monthly budget showing how much you could afford to pay back eack month;
- a list of CSBs or other investments you are willing to use for collateral.

Visit your own bank first and talk to the manager, if you know him/her, or the loans officer. Don't accept the first deal the bank offers. Often you can do better, much better.

If you have been a customer for quite some time, mention that and suggest that the bank officer look up your account or accounts. Use that as a bargaining tool and say that as a good and valued customer you feel that you should be able to borrow from the bank at the prime rate, that is, the rate usually charged to favoured customers. You may not be able to get prime, but you should be able to settle for prime plus 1 or 1.5 per cent. That means that if the bank's prime rate is 11.5 per cent, you should be able to get your loan at 12.5 or 13 per cent. If you can get it closer to 11.5 per cent, congratulations! Banks would prefer that you pay prime rate plus 4 per cent.

You can also ask for an open loan. That means you can pay it off whenever you want without having to pay a penalty.

Make it clear that if you don't get what you want, you will go across the road or down the street to other banks, trust companies and credit unions. Even if the deal the bank finally offers seems good, say you would like to think about it and visit other institutions to see what they would offer. It gets easier as you go along.

Once you have struck a deal, make sure you read all the fine print on whatever sort of contract you are given. If there is something there you don't understand, ask and keep asking until you do understand. Even if you are told that something is "standard practice" you can still ask that it be removed or changed.

Once the bank has agreed to lend you the money, ask that it be put in your account when you need it and not before. Inquire as to the day of the month the interest or interest-and-principal payments are due and make arrangements for them to be taken from an account, if that is easier than trying to bring in cash.

Pay your installments on the day they are due, and add extra bits if you can afford it and if the deal you made allows it. If you run into trouble, explain why you need an extension.

Good luck!

Borrowing from Friends and Relations

Borrowing from friends and family can work out well if — and this can be a large if — everyone concerned is aware that it is a business arrangement. Make sure all the details are worked out and written down with a copy for everyone. That way, there can be no recriminations later. And if things get tough and you can't make all your payments, don't assume that it will be all right to put your loan from a friend or member of the family on the back burner while you concentrate on other debts. Be honest, tell them the situation and ask if you can make other payment arrangements. No loan in the world is worth losing a friend over or having a family member feel that you took advantage of your relationship.

Borrowing Against Your Life Insurance

If you have had a life insurance policy since before September 1, 1968, run, don't walk, to your agent and borrow against the cash value accrued. Up to that time, insurance companies were bound by an undertaking to the federal government not to charge more than 6 per cent on such a loan.

Since then the rules have changed. The companies now promise not to charge "an unreasonable rate of interest" to policyholders.

Let's look at what such a loan could do for you. If you borrowed $2,000 in November 1982 to buy Canada Savings Bonds, you would have had to pay, if you qualified, $2,000 times 6 per cent (the rate of interest charged by the company) which would be $120 a year. If your premium for the year was $60, the total cost to you, interest plus premium, would be $180.

With that $2,000 you could buy Canada Savings Bonds which would

47

earn you $2,000 times 12 per cent (the rate of interest paid by CSBs at that time) which would be $240.

Thus, what you earned on your borrowed money ($240) would pay the interest you owed on the borrowing ($120) plus your annual premium ($60) and leave you $60 in profit.

You would actually be even further ahead because your premium would have had to be paid even if you hadn't borrowed the money. To make things even better, the whole deal cuts your income tax because interest paid on money borrowed to make money is tax deductible.

Don't bother to pay the insurance company back unless there is no difference between the interest rate you have to pay and the interest your money earns. Naturally, when you borrow against your policy, your coverage drops. If you had a $10,000 policy and borrowed $2,000, the coverage at death would be only $8,000 ($10,000 minus $2,000 equals $8,000). But in the long run your heirs have not lost anything because the $2,000 has been invested in something. That, added to the $8,000 insurance, again totals $10,000.

If you have already borrowed on your life insurance, but used the money to make a personal purchase (a car, clothes, furniture and so on), pay it back as soon as you can and then reborrow immediately for investment to earn the tax deduction. It may seem like a duplication of effort but you have to do it this way to prove beyond a shadow of doubt that you borrowed the money to put in a money-generating investment. If they question you, you can wave your receipt for the investment at the feds.

Borrowing this way can give you a quick start on investing. If you borrow the money to invest in Canada Savings Bonds, you can then turn around and use the bonds as collateral to invest in other stocks and bonds and perhaps earn some dividend tax credits. Remember: as long as you invest the money you borrow, the interest you pay is tax deductible!

Renegotiating Loans

If you are paying horrendously high interest rates on a loan taken out in 1981-82, now is the time to try to refinance. Banks are not legally required to allow you to take out a new loan at prevailing lower rates but some are doing so to keep the business. They are even, in some cases, waiving additional charges for early repayment.

Once you've decided to try to refinance, gird up your loins for battle. Bargaining with bank-loan officers is seldom easy but it can be done.

When you talk to the bank official, ask immediately for "prime," the rate at which a bank loans money to its "preferred customers." You probably won't get it but you will get considerably closer than if you accept the rate the bank suggests.

To get what you want, be prepared to prove:

- you have been a good customer;
- you have made all the loan payments on time;
- you would accept repayment over a shorter period of time;
- you are a good credit risk with a steady paycheque and a solid net worth;
- you are prepared to go somewhere else if you can't make a satisfactory deal.

A young woman we know recently attempted to negotiate a reduction in the interest rate on her education loan and was kept waiting for a pre-set appointment beyond her patience and ability (she had to get back to work). Annoyed, she shopped by phone and found that she could get a loan at much lower interest at another bank. She phoned her tardy bank clerk and reported this. He quickly offered her a competitive interest rate and promised to wait for her until she could come in and make the arrangements. There's another lesson to be learned here, and that is, shop around. Maybe you didn't know you could do it with banks. You can.

If you ever think you are being discriminated against because of your sex, holler about it — to the manager of the branch, or if necessary to the head of the whole institution. Money is uni-sexual and shouldn't be coloured by a loan clerk's bias. Don't whine, whimper, wheedle or apologize when you need to borrow money. State your case, parade your collateral and be confident. It's not as if you were asking for blood; it's only money.

6

The Budget

"Budgets are not merely affairs of arithmetic."
WILLIAM GLADSTONE

Budgets and Emotions

Budget is a word like diet; to most people it means deprivation and discipline. Some women think of it as punishment. A friend of ours was pregnant with her first child and she and her husband were budgeting to buy a fridge, stove and washer so they could move into a house with space for the baby. Her husband, who narrowly escaped being an accountant, worked everything out on paper and showed her what they had to live on. She thought he had left out Christmas and burst into tears.

You can get very emotional about figures.

Emotions are what you have to cope with before you can cope with money. You have to realize that you can make money work for you and do what *you* want it to do — that is, if you know what you want. That's why we spent so much time talking about your goals. Making them happen is often much easier than figuring them out. You just have to be clear in your mind. You also have to be clear in your emotions.

A lot of people with good incomes think budgets are for poor people. And a lot of people think budgets are punitive and that they restrict their free spirits. What we need first is a basic approach. For some of you it may mean a complete change of attitude.

Budgets are not to stop you, but to enable you. Budgets are to help you face the end of the month without a queasy feeling in your stomach because you've run out of money before you've run out of bills to pay. Budgets are to make holidays and special events and dreams come true. Budgets are to reassure you, not to scare you. Budgets are to live by, but they're not written in stone.

Four Basic Rules

There are four basic financial rules for income, outgo, savings and insurance that we all should follow — if it's not too late. If you already have a load of debt, and you're paying off loans on furniture or a car or too much indulgence with your credit cards, then we'll have to deal with that later. But here are the rules:

1. Find out exactly what your net income is. Net, not gross.
2. Plan to spend approximately half your take-home pay on housing and food. Recommended percentages a few years back were 31 per cent for housing and 23 per cent for food, but it depends on your base income how the percentages work out. Here's a depressing fact we recently discovered: it costs 20 per cent more to feed one person alone than one in a family of four.
3. Save. This is the hard part, and we'll get to that.
4. Insure. And this opens a world of possibilities, which we'll discuss later. What you do depends on whether you're single with no dependants, a single parent, married, with or without children, at home or working, or widowed, with or without dependants (see chapter 8).

Keep a Notebook

You must know where your money goes. Buy a small notebook and keep track of where you spend money over the next three months. It takes that long to establish a realistic spending pattern. If you try to do it in any less time, you will find yourself postponing purchasing something because it won't look good "in the book."

The three-month record gets you down to the nitty-gritty in short order. Look at where you've spent your money — coffee breaks, movies, haircuts, the extras. They all add up. Until you see the figures you can't decide what is really important and what can be changed to fit the life-style you want to have for yourself and/or your family. *Then* you can set up your budget.

Budget

To budget you need to know:

1. what is coming in (you've already found that out);
2. what is going out (you've listed salary/wage deductions);
3. your priorities (that comes with goal-setting):
   - paying off debts
   - living within your income
   - saving for a short-term goal (perhaps a holiday)
   - putting spending on a cash basis
   - saving for a long-term goal (education, house, and so on).

"Outgo" Lists

To begin with you will have two parts to your budget: income and outgo. You should have one "outgo" section that lists your fixed annual expenses and another that lists monthly expenditures. Your "outgo" lists should, when finished, look something like this:

Fixed Annual Expenses:	
House taxes	$900
Life insurance	200
House and contents insurance	400
Car insurance	500
Total:	$2,000

Monthly total ($2,000 ÷ 12) = $166.67 per month.
Some people like to include other annual expenses in this section, such

as:	Holidays	$1,000
	Gifts	200
	Christmas	400
	RRSP	1,500
New Total		$5,100

Monthly total ($5,100 ÷ 12) = $425 per month.

It's up to you to decide exactly what you want to include in the annual section but you soon find out how valuable it can be. With Christmas bills in January, car-insurance bills in February, house taxes due in June, you can find yourself lurching from financial crisis to financial crisis as you desperately try to find the money to pay the bills. Once you have a budget set up that takes these annual bills into consideration, the pressure is off and life becomes much simpler. Then it's just a case of getting the required amount of money each month into the highest daily-interest savings account you can find so that it mounts as quickly as possible.

Monthly Budget

Here is the breakdown of a sample monthly budget:

Monthly Budget:	December, 1983	
	Budget	*Actual*

Savings:
  Savings account
  Payroll-deduction payment for CSBs

Annual expenses: (divided by 12)
  House taxes
  Life insurance
  House and contents insurance
  Car insurance
  Holidays
  Gifts
  Christmas
  RRSP

Housing:
  Rent/mortgage payments
  Utilities:
    water
    heating
    telephone
    hydro
  Household supplies
  Repairs

Transportation:
  Car payments
  Car repairs
  Car upkeep (gas, oil, etc.)
  Parking
  Licence

Food:
  Groceries
  Eating out
  Liquor/beer
  Cigarettes

Personal Care/Allowances
  Health-insurance plan
  Hairdresser
  Barber
  Cosmetics
  Grooming products
  Medical prescriptions
  Allowances:
    husband
    wife
    children

Clothing:
  Dry cleaning
  Clothes
  Sewing materials

Help:
  Day care
  Baby-sitting
  Cleaning person
  Housekeeper

Education/Recreation:
  Entertainment
  Magazines/books
  Music lessons
  Courses:
    fees
    materials
  Admissions to swimming pool, etc.
  Newspaper subscriptions

Miscellaneous:
  Savings for appliances, furniture, etc.
  Savings for anticipated dental bills

Totals:

Monthly total of actual expenditures:
Take-home pay:
Over/under budget:

If you've done your homework and kept strict track of what goes in and out for three months before you fill in the budget estimates, you won't have to make many changes once you start. However, the three keys to any budget are: it must be (1) reasonable, (2) realistic and (3) flexible. The three months of record-keeping should give you a head start.

No two budgets will be alike. When your children are away from home, long-distance phone bills may be a priority; when they are university age, you may need money to help them pay school expenses; if you go back to work, a new wardrobe may be of prime importance.

Don't be afraid to mix and match your budget. Change it rather than give it up.

Sorting Out The Figures

Some people like to keep money in envelopes and pay expenses from the designated envelope; others have separate bank accounts for separate things; still others pay for everything on their credit cards. It's what works for you that is important.

At the end of every month, transfer the amount you spent on each item to a sheet at the back of your budget book under the appropriate month. At the end of the year you should have 12 separate totals for every entry, which will show you at a glance how you and your budget have done over the past months.

After you transfer the monthly totals, quickly go over your budget once again and make any changes that might be appropriate. If you've paid off your Canada Savings Bonds, you can switch that amount of money into another form of savings; if one child has left home, your grocery bill should be cut; if a family member needs braces, dental bills will look large.

Managing Your Goal Plan

Make a little list each day of what you want to accomplish. Whether it's losing weight, saving money or learning something new, you do it one day at a time. It's the cumulative effect that counts. Don't be discouraged if you slip — a lot, even, at first. Old goals and old habits are firmly embedded. It takes will power to skip the coffee break you've been accustomed to, to brown-bag it when you enjoy lunch out, to fight your way through the financial pages until you understand them.

Know Yourself

Financial planning is a must for everyone, but it's really essential when

56

you're living on a shoe-string and trying to tie a double knot with it. Don't be so hard on yourself that you become discouraged before you've given yourself a chance to get ahead. If life seems less bleak with a date-nut-bran muffin at break time, then go ahead and enjoy. Just don't lose sight of your goals. On the other hand, one of the things mature people are supposed to be good at is putting off present gratification for future pleasure. One woman we know figured out that she spent $750 a year on coffee breaks. That's enough to convince anyone!

Budget Breakers

The price of a new magazine bought on impulse too many times a month could keep you in panty-hose instead. (Read the magazine at the library.) Food expenditures include not only the groceries you take home and the meals you eat in restaurants but also the extra coffees on the job or while waiting for someone, and the peanuts or trail mix to fill up that empty space at 4:00 p.m., or the popcorn in the movie house, and they add up to an astonishing sum. Smoking, of course, is ridiculous, and we won't talk about it.

We have one friend who loves fresh flowers in her house all year round. It's a lovely idea, but it costs a lot to maintain such a habit. On the other hand, you could buy a lot of candles. We know one woman who buys her candles in bulk, all white, at a discount store so that she manages romantic lighting on a tight budget. As we said before, it's a question of priorities.

One Idea is Worth a List

Magazines and newspapers are full of articles about how to save money and there are masses of books in the libraries just waiting for you on how to save money on almost everything you do or buy, eat, read or wear. And you — what can we tell you? — you're already a household manager, no matter what size the household is. What you want to learn is financial planning and that's quite different from household management, isn't it? Yes, and no. But if we're starting at the bottom line, with your base income and how to stretch it, we might as well review a few basic tips about saving money. We always figure that if you learn *one* new idea from lists like these, it's worth it. We'll just hit the high spots, ideas that are really important or that hadn't occurred to us before, and give you a bunch of good titles in our bibliography for you to follow up on if they appeal to you.

Basic Approach

1. Watch like a hawk. "The price of eternal vigilance," said

Marshall McLuhan, "is indifference." We don't think that's true. We think the price of eternal vigilance is eternal vigilance. You can't stop. Waste eats up your money when you're not looking.

2. Don't add new expenses. Book clubs, for example, are some people's downfall. After all, they think, just four books a year. But books are like peanuts. You can't stop. So the trick is not to start. Don't start, join, or agree to anything with an open-ended, continuing expense, or easy monthly payments.

3. Keep your inventory down. We read somewhere that people with full freezers are really suffering from a deep anxiety syndrome. Or maybe it's a fall-out-shelter syndrome: hoard, for the holocaust is coming. Listen, if the holocaust comes, the last thing you need is a year's supply of toothpaste. Who's going to have any teeth? Our point is, don't buy ahead too much. Consider the interest you're losing on that money you've tied up in applesauce. Once, long ago, before health-food stores and food processors and plain peanuts, friends of ours bought a 25-pound pail of peanut butter. There was no room in the kitchen cupboards so they put the pail in an unused closet. Unfortunately, they also had a garment bag of out-of-season clothes, heavily protected with mothballs, in the same closet. They soon discovered that even peanut butter cookies are no good when they taste of mothballs!

4. Keep a lid on your overhead. That is, don't let your fixed costs for housing, transportation, heating and so on become a painful burden. The smaller your basic nut is — that is, the amount you need each month to keep functioning — the better off you'll be. If you think there'll be a family mutiny if you don't get a house with two bathrooms, see if you can put a second basin in the one bathroom you have, or find space for a half bathroom in a closet — near the pipes — or borrow a copy of Lillian Gilbreth's *Management in the Home* and put the family on a workable traffic schedule.

5. Borrow money when you *need* something, not when you merely *want* it. Banks and credit companies are just as much to blame as you are. Banks are recommending loans for holidays now — at heaven knows what interest rate. The fly-now-pay-later attitude has to stop somewhere. Always, always check the interest rate on whatever you're buying on time, and try not to buy at all.

6. Energy, energy, that's all you hear these days, and you're going to keep on hearing it. Face it: energy costs are going to keep on going up and up. If you have a car, walk more, or join a car pool. If you do use the transit, walk more. Turn the heat down, put a sweater on, wash your clothes in cold water, run only a full dishwasher — if you have one. (Did you know a dishwasher uses less hot water than someone washing dishes by hand with a running tap?) Insulate the house more, put towels at the doors and windows in really cold weather. Turn off the air-conditioning; hang the clothes outside. Use small appliances because they use less energy than the stove. If you're using the oven, cook the whole meal in it: meat, vegetables and dessert. The unlooked-for bonus from some of these energy- and money-saving tricks is that you'll feel better. You're using more of *your* energy, that's why.

Food

1. Here's one we really like: *The Financial Times* for March 24, 1980, money section, recommends, among ways to save $1,000 on your food bill, that readers buy the book *Encore: The Leftovers Cookbook*, by Betty Jane Wylie, and stop feeding the garbage can. Of course, we agree! Another book recommended in the same article is *Meat Trade Secrets Exposed* by retired butcher Vernon Lutner, who says you can save 20 to 50 per cent on your meat bills by paying attention to him.
2. Stop eating meat — well, not entirely, because you have to know what you're doing. But try going meatless at least twice a week. Check out *Recipes for a Small Planet* to make sure you get your complete amino acids, and check out young people like two of our daughters who are slim, beautiful walking ads for vegetarianism.
3. Remember that food you slice or cut yourself is cheaper, and so is food you mix from scratch, with the exception of frozen or canned orange juice, bottled lemon juice, commercially baked bread (it's the oven heat that costs so much), frozen French fries, pancake and cake mixes to which you only add water. Bouillon cubes and dry packaged soups are cheaper than canned because you pay less for your own water, and instant coffee costs less than freshly brewed. Some people would kill for their morning cup of freshly roasted, freshly

59

ground, specially blended mix of French Mocha Continental Guatemalan filtered coffee, and who are we to argue? Remember: it's a matter of setting your priorities. One person's cup of coffee is another person's lifeblood.

4. We don't have to tell you to shop the specials, watch the price differences between brand and generic products (sometimes the brands are cheaper), make a shopping list and stick to it, don't shop when you're hungry, don't take an impulsive, untrained friend or child with you, and use coupons.

Miscellaneous

1. Shop discount stores, sale racks, thrift and second-hand shops, dime stores (for accessories, underwear, socks), manufacturers' outlets and retail-clearance centres. We don't have to tell you that either, do we? But how many of you check the boys' and men's departments for cheaper and often better-made clothes? You can get Shetland sweaters and Oxford-cloth shirts for far less than you pay in women's fashion departments.

2. Don't buy *anything*, clothes or otherwise, that costs over $10, without having a demonstrated need. If you have thought two or three times, "I need such-and-such," maybe you do. If you can, wait a day before you buy. If you have left your charge cards at home, as we suggested, you'll have to.

3. Give yourself a *daily* allowance. Carry in your purse only the amount of money you know you'll need that day. This is really helpful when you're on a diet; you can't possibly cheat!

4. We told you not to stock up a year's supply, but it wouldn't hurt to buy the family sizes of some things. They usually are cheaper than so-called convenience sizes. Do your arithmetic, though. Sometimes they fool you.

5. Wash your fine woollen sweaters and silk blouses by hand and cut your dry-cleaning costs. We hate this, and you probably will, too, but it really does save money. You may have bought that gorgeous silk blouse on sale but you soon spend what you saved if you have it dry-cleaned all the time.

6. This is in the *Encore* book: don't throw away the toe-heels of wine. Save them for cooking, marinades or for wine vinegar. And don't throw out bacon fat. Save it and use it for frying hash-browns, onions, frittata.

60

7. Develop your lateral thinking. You know that when you haven't any gift wrap, you can use newspapers — the classified ads or the comics are nice — and coloured yarn. Keep thinking like that. What do you have on hand that you could use instead? There was a funny little poem of nagging slogans that was used to promote the war effort (World War Two, darling) when we were children.

Use it up,
Wear it out,
Make it do,
Do without.

That's the kind of thinking we have to promote again.

8. Did you know that you can dilute shampoo with up to half the volume with water and it cleans hair just as well? You can also get some extra washes out of a detergent bottle by sloshing water in the last quarter of the bottle. Add vinegar to the salad dressing bottle and water to the ketchup bottle and get more bonuses.

9. Use newspaper instead of paper towels to polish your windows after squirting on the glass cleaner.

10. And you don't need glass cleaner, either. Use half a cup of white vinegar mixed with a quart of cool water.

11. In fact, *Chatelaine* magazine for October 1982 described a "cope kit" assembled with $5.61 worth of ordinary items that would perform any number of household chores that we buy expensive, specific products for. The items are white vinegar, petroleum jelly, baking soda, salt and liquid chlorine bleach. Search out a copy of old-time household hints and see what other oldies-but-goodies you can come up with to save money.

12. Postage rates are phenomenal. Telephone rates are going up all the time, too. We're not ones to talk about skimping on postage because we love mail. But you could take most of your bills (gas, power, telephone and oil company) to the bank and pay them there if you have a personal-service plan. (There is no charge for handling if you have such a plan.) You save on postage that way. And write a long letter when you do sit down to write and get more words per penny. As for the telephone, watch for the discount times and do your long-distance talking then. If you dial a wrong number long-distance, be sure to inform the operator so you won't be

charged for the call. As with everything else, check your bill carefully each month to make sure you aren't being charged for a call you didn't make. Computers make mistakes, too, you know, and are much slower and less willing than people to acknowledge them.

Clichés

All the most terrible clichés you ever heard are true, true, true, and if you can make any of them stick with fresh glue, you're on your way.
   "Plan your work and work your plan."
   "A penny saved is a penny earned."
   "Penny-wise, pound-foolish."
   "Money doesn't grow on trees."
And remember: thrift is a wonderful virtue, especially in an ancestor.

7

Savings

"It is easier to make money than to save it; one is expertise, the other self-denial."
T.C. HALIBURTON (SAM SLICK)

What Are Savings?

What you have to understand is the difference between *saving* and *savings*. After that, the hard part is behaving yourself.

See, if you give up cigarettes, you save a lot of money that used to go up in smoke. That's saving. But if you don't consciously grab that money and put it somewhere where it will do you some good, it will still burn a hole in your purse and you'll wonder where it went. What you should do is put it into savings, and that's what we're going to tell you about now.

How to Start

The rule is — the ideal, as they say — that you should pay yourself before you pay anyone else. Take 10 per cent of your paycheque right off the top and squirrel it away. Then use what you have left for frivolities such as food, shelter and so on. If you've never done this, it takes some getting used to. At first it seems impossible, and you know what happens to that money the first time you manage to skim it off. An emergency happens, that's what, and it's gone.

So you should have an emergency fund — cash, CSBs, short-term (30-, 60- or 90-day) GICs (Guaranteed Investment Certificates), or Treasury Bills — equal to one-third to one-half your annual net income. We know this seems staggering, but we're giving you the experts' advice. (You could borrow this amount, if the interest you make on it is more than the interest you pay.) The idea is to keep a bare minimum in your daily-interest account and put the rest in higher-return, non-risk investments.

Canada Savings Bonds

Among women's favourite such investments are Canada Savings Bonds. No matter what you think of the way the country is run (and don't mention the Post Office), the government of Canada is a safe bet to invest in. And the interest rates are relatively high for so sure an investment. The really neat thing about them is that you can get your local bank to co-operate with you and help you buy them, by arranging to have a certain amount automatically removed from your account each month to cover time payments for the bonds you are buying. Automatic savings at their best.

We know one woman who was going through a very trying time with her husband (read affair; his, not hers). She didn't know how much longer her marriage was going to last and she thought she had better do something about salting some money away for the looming future when he would leave her for the other woman. This story has a double happy ending, we're happy to tell you, because not only did our friend end up with a nice little nest egg of CSBs, but she saved her marriage, too, by persuading her husband to go with her to a marriage counsellor. You see, it pays to plan ahead!

CSBs should be the basis for any savings program or investment portfolio for several reasons:

- backing comes from the government of Canada;
- rates of interest are usually as good as or better than rates for other investments and the government has raised CSB rates during the life of the bonds to keep them so;
- CSBs can be cashed by owners at any time, at any bank, trust company or credit union;
- there is a choice of interest: regular interest, which pays a cheque to bondholders on November 1 of each year for the interest due on the principal; holders of compound bonds have interest paid on principal plus accrued interest every year and get the lump sum when the bond is cashed or matures;
- there is a choice of denominations from $100 to $10,000 on compound-interest bonds; $300 to $10,000 on regular-interest bonds;
- CSBs are always worth exactly their face value plus accumulated interest;
- they can be bought on the installment plan through payroll deductions at work or monthly payments at financial institutions;
- CSBs have a 100-per-cent collateral value for loans.

The publicity campaign for each year's issue starts in late September. The bonds should be ordered by November 1 although the government usually allows a leeway of a few days (anything from four to as much as 19) before payment is demanded, without having to pay accrued interest. This means shrewd investors can make a bit extra on interest because most financial or investment institutions selling bonds will take orders any time, but switch the money to pay for them to the Bank of Canada on the last possible day. In this way the institutions pay interest (usually equivalent to the rate offered on the upcoming bonds) from early October through to the day the bonds have to be paid for, and the government also pays interest from the first of November through to the last-payment date.

For example, in 1983 the last day to pay for bonds before interest would be added to the purchase price was November 9. That means you could have left the money for your bonds in your daily-interest bank account or at an investment house paying daily interest until November 9 before the money went to the Bank of Canada. This way you would have earned two lots of interest for the same nine days.

If you cashed in bonds on March 1 of the following year it would work like this:

You would get interest from the government for:

November	30 days
December	31 days
January	31 days
February	28 days
Total number of days the government is paying you interest on your CSBs	120

Your money was actually in the government's hands for:

November	21 days *(you paid for the bonds November 9)*
December	31 days
January	31 days
February	28 days
Total number of days the government actually had your money	111 days

Therefore, you gain nine days of extra interest by merely holding back your bond payment until the last possible moment.

The government has the right to cut off bond sales whenever it wants to, but if you order bonds by November 1 (and most places are delighted to take your orders once the actual interest rate is announced, usually during the first week of October) you are sure to get them, even if you don't actually come up with the money until the final day before interest is added to the purchase price.

The federal government usually announces the purchase limits along with the rate of interest. Total amounts allowed a purchaser have varied from $15,000 in 1981 when the 19.5-per-cent yield was particularly attractive, to $50,000 when sales were not expected to be so heavy. In 1982 the limit was $35,000, in 1983, $50,000. In the fall of 1983 the government also allowed people who had the series which matured then (series 29) to roll-over those bonds into the new issue above and beyond the $50,000 limit. Therefore, if someone had $10,000 of maturing series 29 bonds he/she could add that $10,000 to the $50,000 limit for a total purchase of $60,000 of the 1983 Canada Savings Bonds.

But back to where most women are — buying much smaller amounts!

If you buy $1,000 worth of CSBs each year, don't put all your money into one bond. If you are like most of us and had to cash the whole $1,000 to pay a $200 debt, the rest of the money would also melt away. Buy one $500 and five $100 bonds, or three $300 bonds and one $100 or any combination that comes out to $1,000 and adds to your flexibility.

In years such as 1981 and 1982, when rates have been well above those paid by private-sector institutions, people bought bonds simply to buy themselves time. Rather than investing in CSBs for the long term, they bought them to keep their money safe and earning attractive rates of interest until they could see if interest rates generally were going to rise or drop.

People who bought the 12-per-cent 1982 issue planned to cash their bonds in February 1983 if other rates were higher. When it turned out that GIC and bank account rates then were in the 7- to 9-per-cent range, they kept their bonds. If interest rates had been 14 per cent or more in February, they could have cashed in the bonds and invested in other vehicles. It's called hedging your bets!

Actually, more and more people are using Canada Savings Bonds as a sort of bank account. They clean out their savings accounts of money they know they won't need until at least January 1 of the following year (when you cash in your CSBs within two months of

66

purchase, you get only the principal amount and you have to hold them at least until January 1 to get your principal plus accrued interest) and hold onto them until they find something with a better return. In November 1983 savings accounts were paying 6.25 per cent to 6.75 per cent interest so people put their money into CSBs at 9.25 per cent and found that even over a short term, the return made the move worthwhile.

If you have regular-interest bonds, you get a cheque for the interest every November 1 and a T-4 slip showing what interest was paid. This interest has to be included on your income-tax return for the year. If you chose compound-interest bonds, you would also be wise to report the interest every year. You won't get it, but you can include it, for example, on your $1,000 investment income deduction. That way you won't be hit with a huge tax bill when the bond eventually matures. Write a note to the income tax department to include with your annual return, saying you have chosen to report the interest income on the bonds each year as it is earned rather than waiting until you actually have it in your hand.

If you wait, you will pay tax at your personal tax rate on all the interest that has accrued through the life of the bonds. In some instances that comes to hundreds and even thousands of dollars.

Any financial institution should be able to tell you what interest any series of CSBs is paying. Now that legislation is pending which will make it mandatory to report any and all interest every three years, the information may even be more readily available.

When you buy CSBs, ask about the return through the life of the bond. The 1981 bonds had a return of 19.5 per cent for the first year, 10.5 per cent for every year thereafter; the 1982 bonds had a first year return of 12 per cent with a bottom line return of 8.5 per cent for the next six years; in 1983, the return for the first year (and for the second year of the 1982 bonds) was 9.25 per cent, with a guarantee of at least 7 per cent for the final six years.

At the time the 1981 bonds were issued, the government promised a minimum return of 10.5 per cent on all outstanding issues, so in early 1984 any bonds issued in 1981 and earlier are still earning that rate of return, while the 1982 and 1983 issues are bringing in 9.25 per cent. Obviously, if you have to cash in any bonds, do those from 1982 and 1983 first, as they are paying a lower rate of return than those from the earlier years.

When you cash in a bond, ask about cash bonuses. The government declared cash bonuses for several issues as an inducement for holders to keep their bonds to maturity rather than cash them in — another reason to keep older bonds as long as possible.

Guaranteed Investment Certificates/Term Deposits

GICs and term deposits are basically the same thing, the former offered by trust companies, the latter by banks. Most of them involve putting a certain amount of money away for a term of from 30 days to five years at a specific amount of interest. The lucky people who bought five-year certificates at the 19-per-cent and 20-per-cent heights of 1982 are guaranteed that rate until 1987, while those who put money away for five years at 7 per cent in 1979 had to suffer through high-interest times of the 1982 months knowing that they were getting clobbered.

When you buy a GIC, read the small print. Ask if there is any provision for getting your money out in times of emergency (some allow you to do so but pay a lesser interest rate for the time the money was held), or if you are locked in tightly. One woman we know had her whole life savings of $100,000 locked in at 7 per cent in 1979. When she tried to get it out in 1982, she was told that although she couldn't take it out, she could borrow against it — at 22 per cent!

With both term deposits and GICs it is important to tell the bank or trust company that you don't want to have the money rolled over (re-invested) automatically. Insist on being asked each time whether you want to keep it invested in such a way or would prefer to take it out or change the length of time you opt for. If you don't, the fine print on the contract you sign may say that at maturity the money can, at the bank's or trust company's discretion, be rolled over for an equal period of time. For example, if you had a 90-day GIC maturing to-morrow, the financial institution could re-invest the money for an additional 90 days without asking you.

T-Bills

T-Bills are government-backed treasury bills. They can be bought through some investment houses for $5,000 or more; banks usually handle them in units of $100,000.

The federal minister of finance, through the Bank of Canada, calls for tenders each Thursday on such bills. They are sold to the highest bidders from the chartered banks, the Bank of Canada and investment dealers designated as members of the money market. Other dealers also may submit bids occasionally.

Once the bidders have the bills, they turn around and sell them to clients. There is an active market in T-Bills, and many investment dealers keep them in inventory, offering them at current rates to customers.

If you buy $5,000 in T-Bills, you don't actually pay $5,000. You pay $5,000 less the amount of interest that would be earned to make your money amount to $5,000 at a specific date. For example, if on April 6 you bought $5,000 of T-Bills to mature on April 29, 22 days away (you buy the bills one day and must pay for them within 24 hours, which means that the settlement date, the day you actually own the bills, would be April 7), you would pay $4,975.25. The rate at the time was 8.25 per cent. The amount of interest you would earn would be the difference between the amount you pay ($4,975.25) and the $5,000 you will get on April 29, or $24.75. In other words, you make money by paying only for face value less interest rate. This isn't pie in the sky; it's money in the near future.

If on the same day you bought $10,000 worth of T-Bills to mature July 29, 113 days away from settlement date of April 7, you would pay, for a yield of 8.5 per cent, $9,743.60. In this instance the interest earned over that 113 days would be $10,000 − $9,743.60 = $256.40.

Treasury bills always mature on a Friday, but may be bought and sold any day of the week. Maturities available range from seven days to a year.

T-Bills can form part of an investment portfolio and are a handy way to keep money earning more than banks, trust companies or credit unions are paying and still be completely liquid.

No one issues you a statement for income-tax purposes as to the amount of interest you earn on a T-bill investment, so you will have to keep track of your transactions yourself, although they will probably appear on a monthly statement from your investment dealer.

RHOSPs

One way to save the down payment for a home of your own is to buy a Registered Home Ownership Plan. Introduced by the federal government to help young people save tax-free, RHOSPs can be bought by any Canadian over the age of 17. You can put in up to $1,000 a year to a maximum of $10,000 and hold the plan for 20 years — *if* neither you nor your spouse owns a home. Contribution deadlines are December 31 each year.

The plans are administered by trust companies, banks and credit unions and are a contract between the company issuing them and the person who contributes. All have to be registered with Revenue Canada Taxation.

The annual contributions are deductible from any kind of income when you do your income-tax calculations each year. For example, if you have taxable income of $9,000, you can reduce that figure by $1,000 if you have contributed the maximum allowable to your RHOSP.

The idea is to have money in the plan earn interest, tax-free, so that plan holders can accumulate money faster for a house down payment. If you put $1,000 a year for five years into an RHOSP, your principal would amount to $5,000. At the end of another two or three years the total interest paid on principal plus accumulated interest could amount to an additional $5,000. The higher the rate of interest paid, the faster the money mounts up.

In order to set aside $1,000 a year for a house without contributing to an RHOSP, you would actually have to put away $1,500 a year before taxes if you are in the 33-per-cent bracket. The $1,500 would attract tax of $500 (33 per cent of $1,500) and you would be left with $1,500 minus tax of $500 = $1,000.

If you saved $1,000 from your earnings and put it in your bank account for a house down payment, you would have to pay 33 per cent of the $1,000 earned in taxes, or $330, leaving you with only $670 in house savings. Easier to have an RHOSP and much more lucrative in the long run.

There are special rules governing taxation of the RHOSP contents if you bring them out and don't buy a house. Revenue Canada has the details and its representatives can explain them to you. Ask before you deregister (take the money out of) your RHOSP.

You are allowed only one RHOSP during your lifetime, but if you don't like the way it is being handled by the company you originally took it out with, you can change to another as long as you let the bank, trust company or credit union do the work. If you take the money from your RHOSP from one institution to another yourself, you will be deemed to have deregistered the plan. You will be taxed on the contents and not allowed to open a second plan.

Originally, RHOSPs were for young people saving for their first home, but now older Canadians who have sold their family home and are living in rented accommodation with the thought of perhaps buying another in the future may also qualify to open a plan. Again, check the details with Revenue Canada, as rules and regulations affecting RHOSPs can be changed at any time or by any federal budget.

April 1983 Budget

The 1983 spring budget suggested several changes in RHOSP legislation. In an attempt to help stimulate the construction industry, the government says that people who buy new homes by the end of 1984 will be able to deduct from their taxable income the difference between what they actually have in their RHOSP and the $10,000 limit. Supposedly, that means that if you have $100 in your plan you can withdraw it, buy a new house and deduct $10,000 minus $100, or $9,900, from your taxable income for the year!

The house has to be new; the buyer can't have owned a home (nor can his/her spouse) after 1981, and the buyer must move into the house within a certain length of time.

The budget would also allow RHOSP funds to be drawn out tax-free if they are spent on furnishings, appliances and so on.

The government hopes this new legislation will spur the construction industry; encourage some renters to buy houses and free up badly needed rental space; and stimulate other parts of the economy by giving people the additional tax deductions, and therefore more cash, to put them in the market for big consumer items.

What's the Difference?

If thou wouldst keep money, save money;
If thou wouldst reap money, sow money.

Thomas Fuller said that in 1732. See, he knew the difference between saving and savings. Now you do, too.

8
Insurance

"Money gives a man thirty more years of dignity."
CHINESE PROVERB

Everyone Needs It

You've done so well. There you are, all alone, up on that high wire, dazzling everyone with your footwork, twirling your parasol, surprising yourself with your grace and dexterity. Do you know what you need? A safety net. Not just someone's strong arms to catch you if you fall. What you need is insurance. You can't live without it.

You could die without it. A lot of women do, or with such a small policy that it isn't even enough to meet the final expenses. But you cannot live as long as you're going to without insurance.

"We insure women," writes an insurance official, "but we have not sought for woman as we have man, because of the wretched care she takes of herself, and when we do enrol her, on account of the physical risks which beset woman, we tax her $5 additional for each $1,000 of insurance. The additional tax on women's insurance is also retained in some cases because it is not generally accepted yet that a woman's life has a monetary value."

That was written in 1895. You've come a long way, baby. Or have you? The chief physical risk that used to "beset woman" was childbirth. Once antiseptic was discovered, both maternal and infant mortality rates dropped like a stone. A woman's life expectancy at the turn of the century was about 48 years; now it's about 76 years. But a woman who is 65 today can expect to live another 18 years. Both of us come from long-lived lines of women. Barring a plane crash or

73

car accident, we figure we're wound up to run until we're 90. Take a look at your own family background and figure your odds. Chances are that you are going to go on for a long time — probably alone, and probably poor. That's why you need insurance.

Of course, there are different circumstances and cases for every woman, and these determine her needs and the kind of insurance she should have.

Wife and Mother

"It is not generally accepted yet that a woman's life has a monetary value," according to that turn-of-the-century mothball salesman. The arguments are still going on about exactly how much a stay-at-home wife and mother is worth. A lot, as any widower will tell you. We have seen estimates ranging from $15,000 to $35,000 per year as the value of the unpaid service such a woman provides. Here's an estimate of replacement costs prepared by the American Council of Life Insurance (1978 prices):

Job	Hours/Week	Average Pay/Hour
Seamstress	1.3	$ 3.50
Chauffeur	2.0	10.00
Nursemaid	45.1	2.70
Dietician	1.2	4.00
Food buyer	3.3	2.70
Cook	13.1	3.50
Dishwasher	6.2	2.80
Housekeeper	17.5	4.50
Laundress	5.9	3.00
Maintenance worker	1.7	3.50
Gardener	2.3	3.50

Average 99.6-Hour Work-Week Is Worth $333.69
Income Value For One Year Equals: $17,351.00

None of these lists ever allows for the services of social secretary, fashion arbiter (for teenagers), counsellor, grammar instructor, special-projects assistant, games mistress, hostess or courtesan. Can you imagine doing all that work for love and not for money?

But money is what a widower would have to attempt to replace his wife with in the event of her death. Insurance on her life would cover *final expenses* including the cost of a terminal illness as well as funeral

74

expenses. (We know of one widower whose wife's terminal illness with cancer cost him more than $30,000 in child care and medical expenses.) There should be *mortgage-cancellation insurance* on her life as well as his. We think this is the single most important policy a married person can have — it secures the family shelter. The money that would have been used for mortgage payments can go toward housekeeping and child-care services. Money for *education* should be considered so that in the event of either parent's death, the children's futures will not be ruined.

Pensions, we already know, are a problem for women. If a wife and mother is not sufficiently protected by her husband's pension plan, she may end up with zilch. So she needs *retirement funds*.

Working Wife and Mother

Add to all that work she does at home a job outside the house and you have a woman of steel. According to Statistics Canada, married women form the largest group of all working women in Canada — 2.4 million in 1976. The majority of them are working because their families need the money, not because they are intent on pursuing a career and not because they want the luxuries one income can't buy. A 1982 report on working women in the *Toronto Star* estimated that if all working wives quit, the number of families below the poverty line would double.

The second income has become essential income, part of an economic partnership, and therefore in need of protection. A working wife and mother needs coverage for *final expenses*, plus *family-income protection*. (The average number of hours a man increases his home-help when his wife works is one and a half hours per week. *Someone Has To Do It*, as Penney Kome says in her book of that name.) A home being paid for with the help of two incomes should be protected by *mortgage-cancellation insurance* for the wife as well as the husband. Again, *education funds* have to be taken into account. And since women are still being ripped off by their own pension plans, let alone their husband's, *retirement funds* are a must.

Increasing numbers of women, too, as they pull ahead of the game and find themselves more comfortable than perhaps they had expected, want to do something for their growing children. They like the idea of leaving them an inheritance to help them over the hard parts. A Legacy from Mother. (One of us bought our first clothes dryer and our first television set with our legacy from mother.) Insurance is still the most certain way of doing this — call it an instant estate.

Working Wife

The working wife, even without children, still needs insurance. Money for final expenses, mortgage cancellation, income replacement, retirement funds — all these are important. But maybe it's time to talk about divorce insurance.

No, there's no such thing as insurance against divorce, not yet. Can you imagine what the premiums would be? But we came across a fascinating news item recently. According to Hamilton McCubbin, head of the Family Social Science Department at the University of Minnesota, two-income couples are more likely to split up. Add to that ominous warning a StatsCan population expert's prediction that two out of every five Canadian women married today will be divorced by their fiftieth birthdays. Now think again about divorce insurance.

You could start by asking your husband to assign his life insurance to you (he can do so by writing to the insurance company that holds his policy), so that you are the owner as well as the beneficiary. See, if you're divorced, he can change the beneficiary. If you own the policy you know whether the premiums are paid up to date, and you're thereby able to keep it in force, cancel it, change it and designate the beneficiary. Some divorce settlements now allow the ex-wife to continue as beneficiary in order to guarantee continued support payments in the event of her ex-husband's death. If the ugly fact of divorce creeps up on you, try to include your ex's insurance policy in your property settlement.

We heard of one woman whose marriage was definitely queasy. She took out an insurance policy on her husband's life and named herself as beneficiary. She paid the premiums, of course. As it happened, the man did die, shortly after the divorce took place. His ex considered her policy settlement her own private reward for the years of anguish she had put in. By the way, if there's a named beneficiary, the insurance money passes outside the estate and thus is not taxable as part of the estate. If no one is named as beneficiary, the money goes directly into the estate.

If you take out such a policy, the money is yours, if you outlive your husband. If both of you die, then your children get some extra help. Think about it.

The Single Parent

The number of single-parent households in Canada will increase by 84 per cent over the next 20 years, and of these, 81 per cent will be headed by women. Courts are still normally giving custody of the children to the mother when a marriage dissolves (a softer word than break-up). If you are among that 81 per cent, then you need more life insurance counselling than anyone. If you're terrified, welcome to the club. One of us was left the sole support of her children, singled by death, not divorce.

Maybe you're receiving some child-support payments from your ex, but these are notoriously low and frequently unreliable. (Why doesn't the income-tax department supervise support payments, with the same penalties for evasion as for income-tax evasion?) Unfortunately, women still earn less than men do, so what you need for your children is going to be hard to figure out. But you need all the help you can get. What you need depends on the age and number of your children and on your own age, health and future.

Coverage for *final expenses* is a must. One of us is a member of a memorial society. I have discussed with the children what to do with me when I die. If I'm close enough, they can cremate the body and take it back to Stratford to the double plot where my husband is. If I die out of town, on a trip somewhere, I have asked them to bury me wherever I have stopped. My coverage for final expenses is not enough to justify a one-way trip in a box.

Retirement funds remain a top priority, as they are for any woman.

Mortgage-cancellation insurance would be an excellent thing while there are still young children at home. A paid-up home as part of the estate gives a real feeling of security to children. Life insurance could provide *emergency funds*, too, as a help both to the children and their guardian. We hope you have given some thought to a guardian and discussed it with both the children and their father, sister, grandmother, cousin, friend — whoever is involved. *Income replacement* would be a big help for the guardian and children.

The Single Woman

It used to be that marriage was all the insurance a single woman needed. That was the unwritten covenant. In return for bed, board and lifetime security, she exchanged her name for another's and created his home, raised his children and earned her comfort for her twilight years. No more, as we have seen. Do we have to remind you of that grim statement from the Welfare Council's report, that most poor women who live alone are older than 55? Some of them are low-income women who never married; some are divorced or separated, subsisting on inadequate support payments; the majority are "widows who were left with very little on which to live after their husbands' deaths."

Remarriage is not a solution. Fewer than one in 10 widows remarries. Divorcées do a little better, but it depends on their age. The pool of available (read alive) men over the age of 40 is decreasing and considerably smaller than the number of single women. By the time a woman is in her fifties, the ratio of male to female is such that there simply aren't enough men to go around anyway, and those who do, go around with younger women.

There is one bright, curious fact among these gloomy ones: in the last census there were 500 women in Canada older than 60 married to men 30 years or more their juniors!

That's beside the point. The point is that the single woman must take care of herself because ain't nobody else going to. She should provide *final-expense funds* for herself because it's awfully selfish and inconsiderate of her not to.

Most of all, though, she needs what Sophie Tucker called "good cash," cash to retire on. You will find retirement plans discussed in another chapter.

Single Premium Payments

There are, of course, several different ways of paying for your insurance policy once you have decided what you want. Most people pay the fixed premium in regular installments forever, or for the rest of their lives, whichever comes first. It feels like forever. It is possible to arrange for "limited-payment life insurance." This method condenses the premium payments to a specific number of years; the policy is still for life.

But you can also pay all the premiums in advance in one lump sum. This is called "single-premium life," and in the long run, it will save you a lot of money. Be sure to ask about it, because most agents don't push it.

There are different types of annuity payments and you would do well to discuss them with an insurance advisor.

Children's Insurance

It used to be considered morbid to take out insurance on a child's life and is still considered unnecessary. Who suffers financially when a child dies? But that's not the right question. We know a family who took out an insurance policy on each of the four children when each was little. When the kids reached their teen-age years, the parents had enough money to pay up the policies to the age of 21. As the children came of age they could either take over the policies and continue to pay premiums, thereby increasing their protection, or they could leave them at that and consider them paid-up policies — worth $5,000 each. Not a bad dowry or nest-egg, as the case may be. The neat thing was that when each child reached the age of 21, he/she had a source of money for university tuition. The interest rate for borrowing against their policies was legally set at six per cent while bank loans at the time cost 18 per cent. Other advantages:

- a child who might be declared uninsurable because of health problems in adult years would still have some protection;
- the premiums set when the child was very young remain inexpensive;
- the policy gives the child a start on a lifetime insurance program;
- the parents, by paying the policy off ahead of time, eliminated annual premiums, and the advance payments earned dividends, which added to the cash value of the policy.

It could be argued that putting money in a bank account for a child would yield more actual cash but there would be no protection, no start to a life-insurance program and borrowing would have to be done at the rate of the day rather than at a preset rate. The interest rate for borrowing money against an insurance policy can be much lower than what the banks are asking. Something to think about.

Term Insurance

Term insurance is protection for a stated period of time, usually one to 25 years, or to age 70. If you die within that time frame, your beneficiary is paid the amount of the policy. When the time is up, so is the policy, and the protection.

Term insurance is good for a young single-parent woman who needs to provide for the children in case she dies. Later, when the children are grown and on their own, she needs protection of another kind — a hedge against her own old age and straitened circumstances. (That old lady keeps beckoning us.)

Disability

Disability is a monster that looms large in the back of any woman's mind. At 30, the odds are 2.7 to one that you'll be disabled before you die; at 50, the odds are still 1.8 to one. If you work for a company, you will have group insurance that usually includes some disability protection, but check it out. Find out how much it will cost to increase the coverage. (It costs more for women, because they collect more frequently. You see, we don't die any more; we just stagger on.) It costs a lot, we are told, but if you are the sole support of your family, it may well be worth it.

A self-employed person has no protection she doesn't provide herself. Businesses and health-insurance programs are very quick to remove the divorcée's or the widow's name from their lists. If you are self-employed, or work for a small firm that has no group insurance or medical plan, you will have to sign up for pay-direct medical insurance, and find a dental-insurance plan if you can. One of us was thrilled to be able to join a union (ACTRA) that provided some of the group benefits we were lacking.

If you don't already know, find out exactly what you are provided with at the shop. But don't accept it blindly. One young woman we know says she found out too late that she would have done better with her own retirement plan than with the one included in her company's lump employee-benefit program. As with everything else, it pays to ask questions and to shop around.

Especially with life insurance. Shop the companies for the best deal. Premiums can vary by as much as 150 per cent. Even a few dollars' difference can make a huge difference by the time you add them up over the years you'll be paying them. Make sure you know what kind of policy you're buying. And shop for your agent even more carefully than for the company. Male or female, he/she should be sensitive to your situation and your needs, both present and future. Continuing service is as important as the premiums you're paying.

Annuities

A life annuity is a contract providing periodic payments during the life of the recipient, or annuitant. "Annuities are for the living," according to a useful booklet published by the Canadian Life and Health Insurance Association. *This Business of Life* is available upon request.

"The basic purpose of life insurance is to provide your dependants with a continuing source of income if you die," according to *This Business of Life*. "The basic purpose of annuities is to provide *you* with a continuing source of income for as long as you live after you have stopped working." There! We couldn't have said it better ourselves, so we didn't. An annuity is better than a hot-water bottle to keep you warm, fed, sheltered and human in that last long countdown. The basic idea of a life-insurance annuity is that it insures you against the risk that you will outlive your savings. Both you and the company are gambling. If you win your bet, you have a guaranteed income for life. You should live so long!

80

An *immediate annuity* is just that — instant security. Usually older people buy this type. It's bought with one single lump-sum payment. The income from it starts in one month if it's to be paid on a monthly basis, or in one year if it's an annual payment.

A *deferred annuity* is an annuity under which the income starts later, at a set time — on retirement, usually. This type can be bought either by a single premium or by regular installments during the deferred time. Deferred annuities usually have cash values and provide a death benefit before the income payments start. The owner of the annuity can cash in the policy before the payments begin — unless it's "registered" (see RRSPs page 85). The annuity that interests us and that's a little different from the rest is the *joint-and-last-survivor annuity*. If you have an aging parent dependent on you, or a child who needs extra care, you might be interested in this one, too. It pays an income as long as either of the two people it is designed for continues to live. It usually works on a two-thirds, one-third basis, two-thirds on your life, one-third on the life of the person you want to take care of. It's cheaper to buy for an aging parent than for a handicapped child because the odds are different.

If you're relying on your husband's pension plan (all pensions are really annuities), you should find out whether he has a joint-and-last-survivor option in his pension. Don't assume anything.

As with life insurance, it is important to shop around for an annuity that suits you. Rates change daily and are closely pegged to interest rates. Make sure your agent has the most up-to-date figures.

Medical Insurance

The need for medical insurance is self-evident. If you don't have company coverage, be sure to pay directly in order to protect yourself. Extra coverage for private hospital accommodation, ambulance service, drugs and so on is up to you to arrange through other plans. So is dental care. Check out what your place of business provides and decide what you need.

Home and Car Insurance

Remember when you filled out your asset sheet and we told you you'd be surprised at how much you own and are worth? Well, now think what it would mean if you lost all your goods, or the cream of your crop, in a fire or a robbery. Damage, loss and liability have to be insured against as well. If someone breaks her leg on your front step, you might be liable; that is, you might have to pay for her injury. A friend of ours recently had to have her bathroom replastered and papered after a water pipe bubbled in the ceiling; insurance paid for it, after the deductible amount — but not for new matching bathroom carpet!

There are policies for non-smokers, and we heard that some companies will give a five-per-cent discount if you have a smoke detector in the house. This was more prevalent a few years ago than now; smoke detectors are becoming more common. We also heard that some companies will give a discount on the premium if you haven't claimed in the past year. We checked this out with our insurance agent and he pointed out that replacement-value insurance was more important than discounts these days. It's up to you.

All these considerations apply to home or apartment renters as well as to owners. Contents and fire insurance are a must, but sometimes you're responsible for the walls, too. Check with your insurance agent but, as always, shop around. Costs vary.

You might also want to follow up some companies' claims of discounts for teetotallers if you don't drink. Car insurance is expensive, especially for teenage sons. You do know, don't you, that if your children, male or female, have taken driving instruction at school, their car insurance as drivers is less?

Pay Very Close Attention

It isn't easy to be responsible in all directions at once, but it's worse not to be. With all insurance, our advice follows Murphy's Law: when all else fails, read the directions. *Always read the contract.* Fine print may be hard on your eyes, and insurance policies lack something when it comes to style, but you absolutely must know what you're getting into. That means reading every word, the big print and the small print. If you come across something you don't understand, ask your insurance agent to explain it to you. Write down your understanding of what he/she says and read it back so you both know you're talking the same language. Then file your explanation with your policy. A year from now, if you look at the policy and don't understand again, you have your paraphrase to fall back on. When it comes to falling back on something, it's nice to fall back on sanity and logic.

One more tip: if an insurance agent (male) calls you "sweetheart" or "dear" or looks as if he's going to pat you on your pretty little head, turn and RUN!

9

Retirement

"Don't resign. Wait until you're sacked.
Don't retire. Wait until you're dead."
SIR JAMES DUNN

Fear of Retirement

If only you were allowed to work until you were dead! It would be so much simpler. But you're probably going to live a long time. Women do. And they won't let you go on working. Also, you're going to be tired. Although the average life expectancy of a girl-child born today is 76 years, the life expectancy of a woman who has made it to age 65 today is another 18 years. Are you ready for that?

To be retired is to be unemployed, and don't you forget it. What are you doing about it now? Reading this book, for one. This whole book is really about your future, your retirement and the wherewithal that will enable you to face it. By wherewithal, we mean money.

We're not going to talk about hobbies. What you do with your spare time in the twilight zone is your problem. We're concerned that you have enough money to enjoy your leisure time without worrying about heat and food.

Planning For Retirement

It's never too early to start planning for retirement. Too many people work hard all their lives but when retirement comes, they haven't enough money to enjoy their newly acquired leisure time. Make sure that doesn't happen to you by doing some astute financial planning now.

Smart people in their twenties are already learning how to manage money properly and they're putting some away so they can take early retirement if they choose to do so. Others, over 60, still don't know how they are going to live on what will be coming in at age 65.

No matter what your age, it is never too early, or too late, to plan for a better retirement.

Where Are You Now?

With your up-to-date net-worth statement you can see what you have and what might be turned into cash in the years ahead. Try to work out how much it will cost you to live during your retirement years. Some experts say your cost of living will go down anywhere from 10 per cent to 30 per cent. Your need for clothes drops, transportation is usually cheaper, there are senior-citizens' discounts on everything from bus passes to movie tickets, university courses to haircuts. By retirement, your house is often paid for, there aren't any more car payments to make and insurance policies are all paid up.

But inflation may have reared its ugly head again and the dollar you put away for retirement today may not have the same value when you spend it in 1990 or 2020. It's obvious that you can't nail down exactly what it will cost you or you and your partner to live at the time you retire, but by working out projected costs you can get some idea of what you will need and "some idea" is at least a place to start.

What Have You Got?

What can you count on at age 65? There are several sources of retirement income:

- the Old Age Security Pension
- the Guaranteed Income Supplement, for special need
- the Canada/Quebec Pension Plans (since 1966)

These are all government plans. Then there are:

- employer-sponsored pension plans
- Registered Retirement Savings Plans
- personal retirement plans through investments
- part-time jobs or businesses
- sales of personal possessions, especially collections

Pensions, the Bad News

Although 1.4 million women are enrolled in employer-sponsored pension plans, 95 per cent of them are in plans that don't provide full vesting (that is, they're not portable from job to job) until the employee has put in 10 years of service to one company. Even then women usually receive much lower pension payments than men do because these plans are earnings-related and women on the average earn about 60 per cent of what men do. In addition, younger women tend to change jobs more frequently than do men, leaving their pensions behind them. If they marry and take time off to have and raise children, they forfeit the child-care years. And they are sometimes the most dispensable when it comes to lay-offs. The thinking is that women are working just to get out of the house; they don't really need the money, right? Wrong.

Women are often employed in jobs where they are not likely to be offered pension coverage — part-time, low-paying, interchangeable and unprized. Few company pension plans, except for government ones, are indexed for inflation, so pensioners find payments eroded by cost-of-living increases.

A company pension plan is all very well but don't expect it to buy you all the luxuries you might like to have. Check into your employer-sponsored plan as soon as possible and find out what benefits you can expect, what would happen if you chose to take early retirement and how many years you have to work before your pension is vested.

Retirement Savings Plans, the Good News

Up to two million people (one-third of them women) contribute each year to Registered Retirement Savings Plans (RRSPs). Don't consider them merely a convenient way to lower your income tax this year. Look on them as your future crutch, lifeline and source of dignity. In fact, if you are the kind who likes to declare a sabbatical for yourself every so often, an RRSP can help you to save the money to cover the cost!

Young women just getting started in the working world should put as much into these plans as they can. Later in life if they marry and leave the work force to raise a family, they can withdraw some of the funds to give them "money of my own." If they choose to stay single, a good-sized RRSP can mean early retirement and a more financially secure old age.

Every wage-earner in Canada is eligible for an RRSP, within limits. If you belong to a registered pension plan at work to which your employer makes, or will make, contributions for the year, you are entitled to put into an RRSP up to 20 per cent of your earned income to a ceiling of $3,500 minus whatever payments you have made to the company pension plan. For example, if you have been docked $45 a month all year for the employer-sponsored plan and earn $15,000 a year, you would be allowed to put into an RRSP 20 per cent of the $15,000, or $3,000 minus the total of your pension payments at work ($45 × 12 = $540) = $3,000 − $540 = $2,460.

Every cent of the $2,460 is tax deductible if you put it in an RRSP. And cutting your taxable income by $2,460 can make a big difference in the amount of tax you will have to pay.

Because the $2,460 can earn tax-free money all the time it is in an RRSP, it piles up quickly, much more so than it would if you had invested it outside a plan.

For example, if you are in the 25-per-cent tax bracket and have $1,000 to invest in an RRSP, you will save $250 on your income tax, giving you $1,000 in the plan and a $250 refund. On the other hand, if you wanted to have $1,000 to invest outside an RRSP you would have to make $1,333.32 to do it because one quarter of the amount, $333.33 would be payable in taxes before you could have a clear $1,000.

The earlier you get money into your RRSP the better. Because you have until the end of February in the following year to contribute, most people scurry around in February to dig up the funds for last year's plan. Far better to make this year's contribution in January and have that extra 14 months of interest and/or dividends piling up. If you consciously devote yourself to making the contribution early in the year, you will amass many more hundreds and perhaps thousands of dollars in your RRSP.

There are several kinds of RRSPs — banks, trust companies, insurance companies, credit unions and financial houses will all be delighted to tell you the details of what they have available. Shop around for what you feel comfortable with and remember that you can have as many RRSPs as you like. One man we know is approaching 60, and because all RRSPs must be deregistered by the age of 71 he has 11 plans and is going to deregister one each year and take early retirement.

If you are not happy with your RRSP at one place you can have the holder transfer it to somewhere else — don't touch it yourself or it will be counted as taxable income for that year.

If you are self-employed, you can put 20 per cent of your earned income up to $5,500 into an RRSP each year.

Women at home should suggest that their husbands put RRSP contributions into a spousal plan. This way the wife can build up a retirement income of her own. In later years, the husband often has the RRSP income, the investment income and his own pensions — his wife has only OAS. From a tax viewpoint it would be far better for her to have RRSP and investment income, and for him to have the pensions. Each of them paying income tax on, say, $10,000 a year comes to much less than he would pay if he had to claim the whole $20,000 as his income.

RRSP rules and regulations can change from budget to budget, so check on what's new before you invest. Christopher Snyder's *How to Get the Right RRSP for You* and Tom Delaney's *The Delaney Report On RRSPs* are both excellent books on the subject.

RRSPs At Retirement

When you decide to retire, you will want to look at various options open to you for your RRSP funds. You can purchase an annuity, a Registered Retirement Income Fund (RRIF), or simply take your money out and invest it your own way. The first two options would attract no tax, the third would be fully taxable if you brought the whole plan out at once.

There is a 10-per-cent withholding tax on RRSP funds taken out of plans in lots of less than $5,000; 20 per cent on withdrawals of $5,000 to $15,000 and 30 per cent on $15,000 or more. If you plan to use your RRSP to either supplement your pension after retirement or to finance you while you go back to school, raise a family or travel, plan to bring out the money in small lots.

For example, if you take out $15,000 in one lump, the withholding tax (really an installment payment on your income tax) would amount to 30 per cent of $15,000, or $4,500, which would leave you only $15,000 − $4,500 = $10,500 to spend. Better to take out $4,900 three times for a total withholding tax of 10 per cent of $4,900 × 3 = $1,470. Take that off your withdrawals of $4,900 × 3 = $14,700 and you have $14,700 − $1,470 = $13,230! You may have to pay more than the $1,470 on your income tax the next year, but at least you have the money in the meantime.

Choices

Before you decide what to do when you deregister your plan, spend time looking into alternatives. You may want to buy an annuity — remember to get one that has a guaranteed term of at least 10 years but will pay you for life. That way if you are hit by a bus two days after you buy the annuity, your heirs will get at least 10 years of

87

payment. Wives should ensure that their husbands' annuities have survivor benefits so that the plans will pay out until both husband and wife are gone, instead of stopping at the husband's death if the guaranteed period is past.

Annuities can also be bought to cover you and a child, again with survivor benefits.

A Registered Retirement Income Fund (RRIF) is another option. You can transfer your total RRSP, or part of it, to an RRIF which will pay you out a fraction of its total worth each year. If you are 65 when you take it out, it will pay you one-twenty-fifth of the value (it is considered to have ended at age 90) the first year, one twenty-fourth the second, and so on. Usually the payout is smaller when you are 65 than it will be when you are 90. You will have to decide for yourself if that is the way you want things to be. You can elect, within certain limits, to get larger payouts in the earlier years, so check that out, too.

Many Canadians prefer to take their RRSPs out over a number of years, paying tax on the money as it comes out of the plan. That way they can invest the funds in dividend-paying stocks which provide them both with income and a tax break, or in Canada Savings Bonds or other secure investments.

What you decide to do is up to you but make sure you study all the alternatives as carefully as possible before you take any action at all.

Old Men and Old Women Still Aren't Equal

In 1979, the last year for which such statistics are available, men over 65 in Canada had an average income of $10,062; women, $5,983. That set of figures should help women realize how important retirement planning is for them, particularly when StatsCan's poverty line in a large Canadian city is $9,000 a year for singles, $12,000 for couples.

In 1982, Old Age Security plus Guaranteed Income Supplements — the only two sources of retirement income for thousands of elderly Canadian women — gave a couple a maximum income of $10,084, a single, $5,695.

There's obviously a wide gap between what people who retire today receive and what they need if they don't qualify for Canada/Quebec Pension Plan payments, anything from an employer-sponsored pension plan or have savings of their own in an RRSP, an investment portfolio or a bank account.

By figuring what you may need to live on after you are 65 and what is available, you will be able to determine the extent of your own "gap" and start making plans on how to fill it.

88

Where Retirement Money Comes From

(based on 1979 figures)

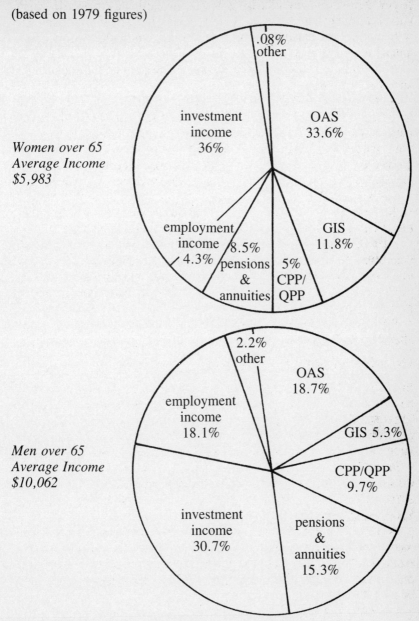

Women over 65 Average Income $5,983

.08% other

investment income 36%

OAS 33.6%

employment income 4.3%

8.5% pensions & annuities

5% CPP/QPP

GIS 11.8%

Men over 65 Average Income $10,062

2.2% other

employment income 18.1%

OAS 18.7%

GIS 5.3%

CPP/QPP 9.7%

investment income 30.7%

pensions & annuities 15.3%

Source: *Better Pensions for Canadians*, Government of Canada, 1982.

Old Age Security (OAS)

Everyone who lives in Canada and is older than 65 is entitled to an Old Age Security pension (OAS) if he/she meets residence requirements. Presently, the government pays a flat-rate monthly pension of $260.52 (as of October 1, 1983), which is increased quarterly, normally by the increase in the cost of living. In 1983 and 1984 the federal government has ruled that such increases will be held to 6 per cent and 5 per cent respectively.

You don't need to have worked outside the home for this pension — age is what counts.

Guaranteed Income Supplements (GIS)

Those who have little or no income other than OAS qualify for a GIS (Guaranteed Income Supplement) from the federal government. Six provinces and both territories provide additional supplements to GIS recipients. All these benefits are income-related and are cut by one dollar for every two dollars of income received other than from OAS.

As of October 1, 1983, the federal GIS was raised to a maximum of $261.55 for an individual whose total income for the year was less than $6,288 or a married person whose spouse gets neither a pension nor a spouse's allowance. A person qualifying for both OAS and the maximum GIS could then count on a maximum of $522.07 a month as of that date from the federal government.

At the same time, the maximum GIS for a couple with an income of less than $9,696, both receiving pensions from OAS, went up to $201.65 each a month, giving them a maximum total of $462.17 each or $924.34 for both as a monthly income. Provincial supplements could increase these amounts.

In 1982, more than half of all Canadians over the age of 65 qualified for some payments under GIS. The monies went to 740,000 women, 480,000 men.

Both the OAS and the GIS are increased quarterly to reflect cost-of-living rises in the previous three months. Although the federal government has said it would keep OAS increases to 6 per cent in 1983 and 5 per cent in 1984 as part of its restraint program, inflation itself has dropped so much that the pension program to date has not been held down by such ceilings.

Total 1983 Income from OAS and GIS

For those over 65 who meet requirements of the two sets of payments, total income from the maximum GIS plus OAS would be $11,092.08 for a couple, $6,264.84 for a single person.

Spouse's Allowance

Spouse's allowances are paid to those between 60 and 65 who are married to OAS pensioners, have little or no income and meet federal government residence requirements. The maximum payment, based on yearly income, was $462.17 per month as of October 1, 1983.

When a pensioner dies, his or her spouse may be eligible to continue to get this allowance until he/she reaches the age of 65 or remarries, depending on his or her annual income.

We Have Seen the Future and It Is Bleak

We called this chapter ''Retirement'' but it could well be entitled ''Self-Defence.'' You want to be sure when you retire that you have enough money to live on, and that it's going to last you. Money is the single most important item that will stand between you and a miserable, poverty-stricken old age.

Poverty is real, also tiring, also humiliating. It's even worse for the aged, and worst of all for the elderly woman, who is usually alone by that time. Until now, women have not been prepared for that devastating time. The old women of Canada need help right now. You who are younger can take steps to help yourselves — right now.

10
Investments

"The Lord in silence works
Towards mysterious ends
The same omniscience lurks
In dividends."
A.M. KLEIN

Before You Start

First of all, let's understand this: investments are not soup. You can't let them simmer on a back burner, unattended. If that's clear, we can go on from there, preferably forward.

The last cheque that cleared the bank before the husband of a friend of ours died was the one paying for a small portfolio of stock he had just bought. Otherwise, our friend says, she might never have dabbled in the stock market. Dabbled — that's the word that is often used, but it's a terrible one. Don't, whatever you do, dabble! This is serious.

Her lawyer arranged the transfer of the stocks to her name and advised her to do something about them when her head had cleared. It certainly wasn't clear when she phoned the wrong city to dump her problems in a strange broker's lap. She had remembered the name of the firm her husband had dealt with, but not the city it was in (she lived in a small town). However, the strange broker was very kind and listened to her garbled, emotional story and invited her to see him and talk. So she backed into the stock market. You don't want to do it that way.

Questions to Ask Yourself

Since we've already established what you want money for, we won't go into that here, but you should ask yourself a few questions before

93

you enter the stock market. Winifred Noble puts them very well in an article in the *Financial Post* (22/11/80):

- Am I the conservative type or do I like to gamble a bit?
- How much can I afford to invest?
- What investment areas would I be most comfortable with?
- Am I clear about my aims and goals?
- Do I want income or capital gain or both?
- Am I the type who would bother my broker unnecessarily?
- Am I a worrier who anxiously scans the stock market pages each day?

Who ever thought you'd have to do a self-administered character analysis before you started investing in the stock market? You thought it was just a broker you had to check out. But if you know the answers to these questions you'll know what to say when/if your broker asks them. He/she has to know your needs, certainly, and the amount you have to invest. But you'll be easier in your own mind if you come to terms with yourself. Investing is a bit like betting the horses when you start: you'd like to break even because you need the money.

What Are You?

- An investor buys a security for a long-term hold (months or years), mainly for income and/or capital gain.
- A trader hopes for capital gain over a period of weeks or months and invests accordingly.
- A gambler or a speculator buys, usually on unfounded tips and after a stock has already gone up dramatically in price, for a short-term capital gain — hours, days or weeks.
- An optimist in the market says one million shares of a particular stock were bought today.
- A pessimist says one million shares were sold today.
- A realist knows one million shares of a stock were traded today.

What Do You Want?

We keep asking you this, one way and another, but it's important. You have to decide what you expect from investing.

- **Income.** If you invest for income, your money should be invested in stocks or bonds that offer regular payment of interest or dividends. This money can supplement your salary or your pension or, if you are a housewife, be for your very own use.
- **Capital gain.** Those who want more money two, five or 10

94

years down the road, or those who don't need additional income now because of their tax positions, often invest in stocks with a capital gain potential. This means they buy the stocks now at what they consider to be a low price, expecting that the shares will increase in value over the years, actually bringing about an increase in capital.

- **Safety.** Investing for safety means that you are most concerned that your capital is not eroded. Usually people who cite safety as a priority want only "blue-chip" stocks (top-drawer stocks such as bank stocks) that can be expected to grow gradually and to return a modest dividend over the years.

Accounts may be in either Canadian or U.S. dollars and most investment houses also give you an opportunity to invest in markets all over the world through their international offices.

Different Kinds of Investments

There are a number of different kinds of investments, and you will be able to choose among them to find out what you're most comfortable with. Now that you have some discretionary money, you are free to do with it as you will. This is the beginning of true financial planning, because now is when you start playing with your building blocks, building your future, or cutting pie (for pie in the sky?). Those are two of the commonest images you'll see to demonstrate where your money should go. The building blocks are actually a pyramid (see illustration).

Consider, before you build yours, the different kinds of investment opportunities available to you:

- government-backed vehicles such as Canada Savings Bonds and Treasury Bills;
- Guaranteed Investment Certificates or term-deposits — issued by various financial institutions for a set period of time with a set rate of interest;
- stocks and bonds.

These will all be discussed in detail. Just be sure to remember Rose's First Law of Investments: "One should never invest in anything that must be painted or fed."

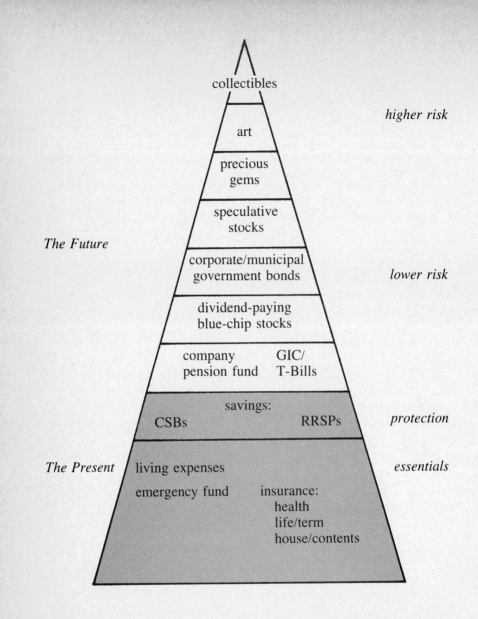

collectibles

art

precious gems

speculative stocks

corporate/municipal government bonds

dividend-paying blue-chip stocks

company pension fund   GIC/ T-Bills

savings: CSBs   RRSPs

living expenses

emergency fund   insurance: health life/term house/contents

higher risk

The Future

lower risk

protection

The Present   *essentials*

The base of the pyramid (shaded area) is made up of the essentials everyone should have before she makes her decisions about the dispersement of her discretionary money. This money is what will make all your budget restrictions and all your funny little penny-pinching schemes worth while. The upper levels in ascending order are more arbitrary and personal (and risky).

Basic Rules

There is no seller without a buyer, no buyer without a seller, because there must be two sides to every transaction. If there are no shares for sale, there can be no buyers; if no one wants to buy shares there can be no sellers. There are some other basic facts you should know because they affect not only your income but also your income tax. For example, you should know the difference between dividends and interest.

What is Interest?

Interest is what you earn on bank, trust-company or credit-union savings accounts, Canada Savings Bonds, Guaranteed Investment Certificates (GICs), term deposits, mortgages, and on corporate government and municipal bonds. In each case you lend your money for a specific length of time for a specific amount of interest — that is, your price for the loan.

What Are Dividends?

Dividends come when you buy shares in a corporation. As a part owner of the company you participate in profits. Dividends are your share of what the company makes.

The difference between dividends and interest is that in one case you are a lender; in the other, you are part owner of a corporation.

Interest versus Dividends

Interest at 11.75 per cent or 12.25 per cent sounds great — not quite as good as 1981's 19 per cent or 19.5 per cent, but decidedly better than dividends of 9 per cent or 10 per cent. But as always, things are not necessarily what they seem. For most taxpayers, because of the dividend tax credits, a 10-per-cent dividend rate is equivalent in after-tax dollars to 15 per cent in interest. So check out the final results before you invest.

Capital Gains and Losses

If you buy shares for $10 each and later sell them for $15 each, you have made a capital gain of $5. If, on the other hand, you disposed of the shares at $5 each, you have a capital loss of $5 per share.

Capital gains occur when you sell something for more than you paid for it. Capital losses happen when you sell for less than you paid. For income-tax purposes there are different classes of gains and losses: personal-use property, securities, listed personal property, and so on.

If you make a profit when you sell stocks or bonds, one-half of it

97

is taxable. If you lose money, one-half of the loss is deductible. Capital losses can also be used to a maximum of $2,000 to offset other income (meaning you would have had to lose $4,000 of which one-half is deductible), and if your loss is more than that you can carry it back one year and amend last year's income tax as well as carry it forward several more years for losses on future years' taxes.

Paper Profits

Some shareholders tend to say they have "made" or "lost" money on a stock when in fact they haven't yet sold the stock. They actually have only a paper profit or loss because they don't have the money in their hands. It's possible you won't make this error in thinking because, as novelist Joyce Carol Oates says, "women only understand money when they can see it."

Both sides of a transaction must have taken place before there is a real profit or loss. It's always better to have cash in your account than to count on paper profits. Don't be like those Carolin Mine shareholders who watched their stock go up from less than $2 per share to more than $50 and then held it while it went down again to $7.

To avoid that sort of situation, try selling half your holdings to realize real profits and holding onto the other half in case there is more capital gain. To do this you would have to buy shares in lots of 200 or more. Then as the price goes up you can consider selling bits and pieces. Once you have covered your initial cost, everything else is pure profit.

Investment Income Deduction

When you do your income tax each spring you'll find the first $1,000 of investment income — interest, "grossed-up" dividends (more on that shortly) and/or capital gains — is tax-free. After that, interest and capital gains (remember that only half of what you make in profit or an investment is taxable) are taxed at your personal tax rate; dividends earn you a dividend tax credit (more on that, too).

It makes sense to get the first $1,000 quickly and painlessly. GICs, term deposits, Canada Savings Bonds all pay good rates of interest and are excellent vehicles.

After you have the $1,000 accounted for, take a good look at dividends and the tax credit they can earn for you.

Dividend Tax Credit

In 1971 the federal government came up with the tax credit from dividends. They did so for a number of reasons:

- to eliminate double taxation on dividends (the corporations paying dividends were taxed before the money went out and the dividend recipients were taxed on their share);
- to encourage us all to buy shares in Canadian companies (at the time, foreign ownership was at an incredible high);
- to provide some relief from the effects of inflation on investment income.

In all cases the dividends eligible for a tax credit must be earned from Canadian tax-paying corporations. They can be paid on either common or preferred shares and some are even paid in U.S. dollars but they must originate with a Canadian-based company.

If you look at the following chart (which illustrates the situation in British Columbia in 1982), you can see how much money you can save if you invest in dividend-paying stock as opposed to interest-paying bonds or term deposits. The chart refers to interest, dividends and capital gains after the first $1,000 in investment income has been earned. It excludes existing federal tax reductions and any provincial credits and/or surcharges that might exist where you live. Any amount over 100 per cent is a credit against taxes payable on other income.

1982 Taxable Income	Marginal Tax Rate	After-Tax Retention			Dividend/ Interest Ratio
		Interest	Capital Gains	Dividends	
	%	%	%	%	
$4,448– 6,672	25.9	74.1	87.0	110.1	1.5
6,672–11,120	27.4	72.6	86.3	107.9	1.5
11,120–15,568	28.8	71.2	85.6	105.8	1.5
15,568–20,016	33.1	66.9	83.4	99.3	1.5
20,016–31,136	36.0	64.0	82.0	95.0	1.5
31,136–53,376	43.2	56.8	78.4	84.2	1.5
53,376 and more	49.0	51.0	75.5	75.5	1.5

By finding your approximate taxable income on the left-hand side of the chart (if you don't know what it is likely to be refer to your last year's income tax form and use the taxable figure from there to give you a rough idea), you can see what your *marginal tax rate* (federal plus provincial) is and what percentage of *interest*, *capital gains* and *dividends* you would get to keep after taxes.

For example, if you have a taxable income of up to $6,672 and earn $100 in interest, you would pay $25.90 in income tax on the money, leaving you with $74.10 after-tax dollars. If your $100 came in capital gains, you would be taxed one-half of 25.9 per cent and would have $87.00; with $100 in dividends income, you would get the whole $100 and have $10.10 to write off against other income.

By following the chart down to a taxable income of $53,376, you can see that in every tax bracket dividends give you a better return than does interest, with capital gains catching up only in the highest bracket.

The final column labelled *dividend/interest ratio* gives you a "magic number" which you can use to determine dividend-interest equivalents. For example, in 1982 CSBs paid 12 per cent. If you wanted to know what dividend you would have to earn to equal that in after-tax dollars, you simply divide the 12 per cent by 1.5 and find that 8 per cent dividend is what it would take.

Conversely, if you are getting 10 per cent in dividends and want to know what that is equal to in terms of after-tax dollars you multiply the 10 per cent by 1.5 and find that it is equivalent to 15 per cent interest.

It is the dividend tax credit that makes dividends so attractive. It works like this: for every $1.00 you get in dividends, you must "gross up" your income by $1.50. Don't ask why: it's just the way the government has decreed it will be. So, if you earn $100 in dividends over a year, you would declare $150 in "grossed-up" dividends as part of your income. Thirty-four per cent of your original dividend ($100 x .34 = $34.00) becomes your dividend tax credit, deductible right off your taxes, not just your taxable income.

In other words, if your tax bill is $1,000 a year and you earn $100 in dividends the $34 dividend tax credit cuts your tax bill down to $1000 − $34 = $966.

You don't even have to do the arithmetic. Companies paying dividends send out T4 forms, which show your grossed-up dividends and your dividend tax credit already worked out so all you have to do is put the figures in the appropriate places on the form.

Interest, Dividends and Capital Gains in Ontario, 1983

Here's an example, courtesy of Dominion Securities Ames, Ltd., of what happened in Ontario in 1983 as far as interest, dividends and capital gains were concerned:

1983 Taxable Income	Marginal Tax Rate	After-Tax Retention		
		Interest	Capital Gains	Dividends
	%	%	%	%
$4,716– 7,073	26.6	73.4	86.7	110.4
7,074–11,789	28.1	71.9	85.9	108.1
11,790–16,505	29.6	70.4	85.2	105.9
16,506–21,221	34.0	66.0	83.0	99.3
21,222–33,011	37.0	63.0	81.5	94.8
33,012–56,591	44.4	55.6	77.8	83.7
56,592 and more	50.3	49.7	74.8	74.8

Again, as for the other chart, tax credits, surtaxes and the $1,000 investment-income deduction are excluded, and any amount over 100 per cent is a credit against taxes payable on other income.

Dividends Save Money

The tax credit means that a taxpayer who gets all her income in dividends can earn more than $40,000 a year and pay no tax because the credit balances off the taxes payable. The catch is, of course, that you have to have a considerable amount of money to invest to pull in more that $40,000 a year in dividends. On the other hand, if a lesser amount was used to get the same amount in interest, or if someone earned that amount in wages, the tax bite would be considerable, cutting your spendable dollars drastically.

The idea that dividends can be better than interest is hard for most people to grasp. It certainly looks as if 14 per cent in interest is better than 10 per cent in dividends, but don't be fooled. Figure out your after-tax dollars, the amount of money you have in your purse after your taxes are paid, before you make investment decisions.

Remember, too, that dividends are normally constant; interest rates fluctuate. Dividend-paying stocks can also earn you capital gains; interest-paying investments can't.

So watch out. Be aware. Don't fall for gimmicks or large signs boasting of high-interest yields. Sit down with a pencil and paper and figure out your approximate taxable income. Work out for yourself what happens when you put your money where. When you have done the figuring, make a decision. Decide what is best for you in your never-ending battle to keep up with inflation and cut your tax load.

Easing into the Stock Market

A lot of women we know have formed small investment clubs so they can learn about the stock market together. Each does her own survey and makes a presentation, stating why she thinks the group should invest in a certain stock. The members' dues form the nest egg to invest, but they can decide to augment their kitty if they want to take a flyer. Any way you look at it, their load is lightened. They don't stand to lose too much money; they're delighted when they make some, and they learn something along the way.

But you might learn faster, and make more money, if you're willing to gamble by yourself. You can start by spending nothing. Well, a little. Buy a newspaper. Read the financial section — regularly. Find out what people are worrying about. That means you'll have to read the front page, too. Watch what's happening in the daily stock-market quotations.

First of all, you have to figure out the code letters of the stock you're interested in. Some of them are easy, some are not. Then you read across the column to find out what happened to that stock yesterday. You will get the industrial average, the high and low it reached and the closing figure. In each case, the figure is the price per share of the stock.

A Phantom Portfolio

Now make up a phantom portfolio. In a sense, that's what happened to our friend who backed into the stock market by accident. The portfolio her husband had bought was almost a phantom. The stock market took a real dive right after he died and didn't recover for a year or so. Our friend simply pretended that the money the stock represented didn't exist, and forgot about it. As money, that is. But she knew the names and the codes of her stocks, so she started reading the market reports to see what was happening to them. Slowly, she started to learn something. You can do this with make-believe stock, for starters and safety, although you won't be nearly as conscientious and attentive as you would be if you had some real money invested in it.

Pretend you have, say, $5,000 with which to buy some stock. Pick a portfolio; a hundred shares of this, a hundred shares of that. Or maybe, if you picked expensive stock, you only get a hundred shares of one thing. No matter. Make a note of what you paid for it when you decided to buy it. Then watch the price as it fluctuates and see what happens to it. If it goes down, down, down, too bad. If it goes up, watch it and decide when you want to sell it. If you sell it for more than you paid for it, you have made a profit. We hope for your sake you don't make too much of a profit right off because that's dangerous. It could not only go to your head, like winning at the races, it could hook you and give you unreal expectations.

When you're ready to invest real money in the stock market, we have two pieces of advice. One is: pretend you don't have the money any more. Consider it a loan to your future and let go. Two: find a really good broker.

Finding A Broker

Once you have decided to invest in the market, your first task is to choose a broker. It's vitally important to feel comfortable with your broker, comfortable enough to say no if you feel his/her advice is wrong for you, comfortable enough to ask questions without feeling dumb. Some women prefer other women as their brokers but there are many men in the industry who treat women clients as people and not as something to pat on the head and tell what to do.

To get a broker you will be happy with:

- talk to your friends and find out about their brokers;
- take courses at local universities or community colleges given by brokers;
- attend seminars or courses sponsored (usually free) by various investment houses;
- drop into brokerage houses and ask to speak to a broker. If you do, remember that new broker's clienteles are built up by steering all drop-in traffic to the newcomer's desk. If you want someone with experience, say so and feel free to ask any broker about his or her background, training, interests, etc. After all, this is the person who is going to be helping you handle your money, and if his or her number-one priority is selling mutual funds and you aren't fond of mutual funds you need to know about the possible conflict of interest.

A Good Broker

A good broker should be able to tell you why it would be good for you to buy a particular stock at a particular moment. A good broker is also honour-bound by his/her professional code of ethics not to sell you something unsuitable for you. If you are a lorn widow or a struggling divorcée, then a broker has no business selling you shares in a wildcat oil company or a sweet film deal. He/she knows that, but you should remember it, too. On the other hand, don't let him/her err too much on the side of caution and put your money in investments so safe that you might as well put it in your sugar bowl for all the money they're earning you.

You may find more than one broker with whom you would like to work. Fine. There's no law saying you have to have only one. Having more does have some advantages:

- each will send you research and information, which adds to your knowledge and choices;
- each will have a different point of view — add them together and you may develop a better over-all picture of what is happening in the market;
- different investment houses underwrite (bring to market) different new issues of stock and by having more than one broker you have more chances to buy new issues;
- you have an opportunity to judge performances.

But don't spread your investments too thinly. If you decide to try two brokers, you may find after a fair trial you are more comfortable with one, or that one consistently outperforms the other, or that it is just too much trouble to remember which stock you have where.

Churning

Beware of churning. Churning is undue activity on the part of your broker, buying and selling so much that he/she is making more money on commissions than you are on profits. You can tell at a glance from your monthly statement if it's happening. Holler about it. Most investment companies claim they monitor their brokers very carefully for this practice, but it won't hurt for you to watch carefully, too.

Opening An Account

This is easy. In fact, you can do it over the phone rather than in person, if you prefer, and if you have previously had a long talk with the broker. Surprisingly enough, there is nothing to sign and nothing to pay, just a few relatively simple questions to answer.

It is important that you are totally open with your broker. Before you open an account, spend time with him/her and clearly outline your financial position, explaining your resources and your goals. Now is the time to discuss whether you are an investor, a trader or a speculator, whether you prefer to be in the Canadian market or another one, if

104

dividends are important to you as a means of cutting your income tax.

Once you have settled in your own mind the type of investing you want to do, it is time to open an account. You will be asked your legal name, address, phone number, the name of your employer, your occupation, your annual income, approximate net worth, goals (are you investing for income, safety or capital gain?), your level of investment knowledge and whether you will be entering your own orders. Sometimes husbands and wives sign agreements allowing each to order stocks or bonds in the other's account. Husbands and wives may opt for a joint account or for one that has a "right-of-survivor" designation. That means that if one person dies the securities are automatically registered in the other person's name without having to go through the estate.

Be scrupulously fair. Don't tell your broker you want to concentrate on capital gains and then complain because you aren't told about new income issues.

It costs nothing to open an account but you may be told that it is the investment company's policy to require you to pay for your first purchase before your order goes in. Others ask for only a payment on account.

Most brokers will ask whether you want your certificates (the formal pieces of paper that say you own a particular number of shares of a particular company) registered in your name and sent to you, or kept by the investment house. If you opt to take them yourself, keep them in a safety-deposit box and remember that when you sell, it involves a trip to the box and to your broker to make sure the certificates are turned over within a five-business-days period so the deal is completed and you can claim the money from the sale.

You may have your dividends and interest sent to you, to your bank, credit union or trust company or kept in your account, whichever you prefer. Most accounts pay daily interest credited monthly with rates competitive with other financial institutions and some clients use them as they would a bank.

How Much Money Is Enough to Start?

Some brokers insist that you have a minimum of $5,000 before you start to invest; for others, $500 to $1,000 is enough.

Coffee Breaks Will Never Be the Same

We'll tell you one thing: once you get hooked on the stock market, your coffee breaks will never be the same. You never knew what a pleasure a conversation could be until you started discussing stocks and bonds. Suddenly you will take a greater interest in the front pages of newspapers than you ever did before, because what happens in the world affects the stock market and your investment in it.

In our kitchen life we knew stock only as the base for soup. It has taken on added seasoning since we broadened our base of understanding. Stock is not soup, but you still have to watch the pot!

11
Your Portfolio

*"Miller's Law: Unless you put your money
to work for you — you work for your money."*

Where Are You Going to Put It?

Have you noticed how attractive briefcases are these days? Since women
have started carrying them, designers have laid themselves out to create
masterpieces of fine leather with handsome trim that are neatly un-
derstated. It's because — at last — women have something to put in
briefcases.

Actually, they're for business papers. You can't put your bonds or
stock certificates in your briefcase; it's not safe. Unless you want to
turn everything over to your broker to administer, you'd be well advised
to keep these papers in a safety-deposit box, with a complete and
accurate record of what's in there. Now the question is: *what* are you
going to put in there? It's called a portfolio.

What is a Portfolio?

When you list your Canada Savings Bonds, your term deposits, your
Guaranteed Investment Certificates, any mortgages you may hold,
stocks and bonds that you own, the total becomes a portfolio. Some
people also include gold certificates, bullion, precious gems and collectibles. The latter won't fit into a safety-deposit box and often need
dusting.

How Diverse Should a Portfolio Be?

In these uncertain times, many people don't want to have all their eggs
in one basket. So they spread their money around. How much spreading

you do is up to you and depends on the time you have to look after what you have.

How Do I Start To Build A Portfolio?

If you have any Canada Savings Bonds, a term deposit, a GIC or any stocks or other bonds, you already have started your portfolio.

Basically, because of the $1,000 investment-income deduction (the first $1,000 you earn in interest, "grossed-up" dividends and/or taxable capital gains is tax free), you should start any portfolio with high-interest bearing investments such as CSBs or GICs. Once you have your first $1,000, or if dividends are bringing in as much as interest, look at dividend-paying stocks, especially if you are concerned about safety or cutting your income tax through the dividend tax credit; concentrate on common stocks if you prefer to try for capital gain. Read on for explanations!

If you have $5,000 to invest, start off buying $5,000 worth of CSBs. That would have given you in 1983, an interest income of $5,000 x 12 per cent (the interest rate from November 1, 1982 to November 1, 1983) = $600. If you had had another $5,000 to invest in the fall of 1983 you might have considered putting $3,000 of it in the 1983 series of CSBs. If you had added the $600 interest to the $3,000 your total CSB holding would have been $8,600 and your interest for the year, $8,600 x 9.25 = $795.50 as of November 1, 1984.

The other $2,000 could go into a preferred stock paying 10 per cent in dividends. That would earn you $200 in income and a dividend tax credit of $200 x 34% = $68, which can be deducted from your income-tax bill for the year.

A third-year investment of $5,000 could go into another preferred stock ($2,000), plus a certificate for some silver ($1,000) plus some common stock with capital-gain potential ($2,000).

It isn't likely that the average person has $5,000 to invest every year, but at least a plan like this does show you some alternatives.

What Kind of Stocks Are Available?

Stocks come in a variety of forms. The vast majority of shares are designated as *common*, which means those who hold them may or may not get a dividend. In case of bankruptcy these shareholders would probably be on the bottom of the pile of creditors. Common stocks are touted as the kind to buy if you are looking for capital gain. However, as with every rule, there are exceptions. Bell Canada, common, for example, is basically a very stable, stodgy investment, usually bought not for capital gain (although sometimes it does provide one) but for income. The company prides itself on trying to raise its common dividend each year by the same percentage as inflation.

Other stocks are called *preferred*. These normally have a stated dividend that is constant and that is included in the name of the issue. For example, "Bell $1.96 preferred," or "Transalta Utilities 14.25% preferred" — in each case the dividend is mentioned. For the first, the actual dividend is spelled out: $1.96 for the Bell per share. In the second instance, the dividend rate is 14.25 per cent of the issue price, which in this case was $25. Therefore, the per-share dividend for that particular issue would be $25 × 14.25 per cent or $3.56 per year.

Some preferred are *plain preferreds*, which means they go on ad infinitum paying the same dividend and going up and down in value as the market moves. Most suffer when interest rates rise. For example, a preferred that was issued some years ago at $20 paying 5 per cent would not bring $20 in the current market when a 10-per-cent yield is more common. In fact, the original $20 share would probably sell for about $10 these days. That way, the original 5-per-cent dividend would now be about 10 per cent of the current price. If that's confusing, back up a bit. Remember that the dividend is 5 per cent of the original $20 purchase price, or 5/100 × $20 = $1.00. That return remains constant. When the price of the stock drops to $10, the dividend still pays a certificate holder the one dollar, but on the $10 price, and the return would be $1/$10 or 10 per cent. Thus, preferred stocks with fixed dividends tend to move down as interest rates move up. Nobody wants to pay $20 to get one dollar in dividends, but if the rate is competitive she might pay $10 per share to get the one dollar. When interest rates move back down to the 5-per-cent range, the stock price will have moved up so that the original purchaser is more likely to get her $20 per share back.

Partly because of this, Canadian companies are now issuing what are called *retractable preferreds*. These shares come out at a specific price, say $25, pay a specific dividend, perhaps $2.50 (10 per cent) and are retractable. That means that whoever holds them on a specified date in the future can, at her option, ask the company for the original price of $25 per share back. It is the retractable provision that makes these stocks so attractive: buyers know what they cost today, what the dividend is and how much money is due at retraction. It's almost like having a term deposit that pays dividends.

Convertible Preferreds

Another kind of preferred share, which has proven to be very popular (and lucrative) over the years, is a *convertible preferred*. When you buy one of these shares, you are also buying the right to "convert" the preferred into a certain number of shares of, or a certain part of, a common stock.

There is a Royal Bank convertible (and retractable) preferred. It was issued at $25 per share, is retractable at $28.75 some years down the road, and it can be converted on a one-for-one basis for Royal Bank common stock on payment of an additional $5 per share.

The Husky Oil 13-per-cent convertible can be changed into four common Husky shares any time up to July 1992, while the Noranda convertible preferred can bring you 2.75 shares of the common for each preferred up to June 15, 1987.

To some investors a convertible preferred that is also retractable is the best of all possible investments because you know what you could get at retraction date, you have the conversion option and usually the shares pay a reasonable dividend.

Cumulative and Redeemable

When you are considering buying preferred shares, the words *cumulative* and *redeemable* are important to understand. When a preferred share is described as cumulative it means that if for one reason or another the dividend is "passed" (not paid), the amount of dividend to be paid accumulates. Some shares have passed dividends several times in succession and then paid off the accumulated total, creating a bonanza in dividend tax credits for those holding the shares at the time the dividends are paid out.

A "redeemable" share is one that a company, at its option, can redeem (take back at a certain price) at times stated in its prospectus, which comes out when a stock is first issued.

How Much Will It Cost?

Every time you buy or sell a stock or a bond you pay a commission to your broker's company. Set by the Toronto Stock Exchange, the commission rates were the same across Canada for many years. Then, in the spring of 1983, discount brokers were allowed to operate. As order-takers and executors only, these brokers can discount commission charges but offer no advice, background information, research services, safe-keeping of securities or new issues.

When the discounters became legal, many of the old, established

110

firms jacked their commission schedule 10 per cent above the TSE rates and then offered a 10-per-cent discount to clients placing large orders.

Most clients stayed with their old brokers because they liked the full-service concept and also because they appreciated the opportunity to buy new issues underwritten by these houses as they came to market. New issues of stocks are big business. Hundreds of millions of dollars are raised each year by underwriters as Canadian companies issue new stock to pay for expansion, research and development or debt repayment.

Full-service companies can order new issues for clients who find that buying them can lead to good profits. Sometimes, of course, the stocks go below their issue price but usually the solid, blue-chip ones make a profit for their original buyers, often within weeks or months.

Two other advantages to new issues are that there is no additional commission to pay (the commission is built into the original price) and that there is usually a two- to three-week period (or even longer) before the shares have to be paid for.

The Toronto Stock Exchange Commission Schedule

Even the companies that have upped their commission use the TSE as a base model. The actual amount a client pays depends on the total value of her order and, for stocks that cost more than $5 each, the number she buys.

- Shares trading from 1¢ to $4.99 each generate a commission of 3 per cent of the total value of the order.
- Shares trading from $5 to $14.99 generate a commission of 2 per cent of the total value of the order plus 5¢ a share.
- Shares trading for $15 and more generate a commission of 1 per cent of the total value of the order plus 20¢ a share.

It sounds confusing but it actually is quite simple to work out:

Buy: 2,000 ABC @$1.50 per share:	$3,000
Commission: 3% × $3,000	90
Total cost:	$3,090

Buy: 300 XYZ @$10 per share:	$3,000
Commission: 2% × $3,000	60
Plus .05 × 300	15
Total cost:	$3,075

Buy: 100 LMN @ $30 per share	$3,000
Commission: 1% × $3,000	30
Plus .20 × 100	20
Total cost:	$3,050

If your order to buy or sell involves more than $5,000, there is a tapering of commission that any stockbroker can explain. (If the company you deal with has raised its rates by 10 per cent, add that percentage to the above calculations.)

Most investment houses charge a minimum commission of $35 to $45 per order. This means that if you order only $200 worth of stock, your commission would be a minimum of $35 to $45. Obviously, it pays to place orders involving larger amounts of money so that the commission doesn't play such a large part in the total cost of the transaction.

Transactions

Each transaction generates a contract, which is sent to you, advising you either of the total cost, if you have bought some stocks (cost plus commission), or of the net proceeds, the amount of money the stock sold for minus the commission. Normally, orders are entered in "board lots" of 100 shares. If you have an odd number to buy or sell, you may find it costs more to buy in or brings you less on a sale.

For example, if you try to sell 146 shares of ABC at $6, you might easily get rid of the 100 at your stated price but the 46 could sell for only $5.85 or $5.75 per share. On the other hand, if you wanted to buy 54 more shares to bring your holding up to a normal 200 shares (146 plus 54), the extra 54 would probably cost you $6.125 or $6.25 each.

All shares bought must be paid for within five business days which, because of weekends, stretches out to seven days. If there is a holiday within that time you get an extra day to pay. Conversely, when you sell shares, the money is not made available to you for five business days. The time is set to give investment houses an opportunity to process contracts, mail them out and accept payment. Unfortunately, sometimes the contracts don't arrive until after the money is due. In that case, a buyer, even without a contract, is liable for the cost of the stock plus commission. A brokerage house can charge interest on what is overdue. Unfair? Maybe, but legally binding.

112

ISIPs

Indexed Security Investment Plans (ISIPs) were mentioned in the 1982 budget and studied by a committee of business and investment leaders who made the recommendations written into the 1983 budget speech.

In effect, the plans have made tax exempt the inflationary part of capital gains on common shares in Canadian companies publicly traded on Canada's five stock exchanges.

The plans were open to some trusts and any individual on October 1, 1983, after the finance department hammered out final details, again in consultation with experts across the country.

ISIPs are administered by banks, trust companies, credit unions, mutual funds, insurance firms, investment dealers and brokers. They can include common stock and some rights, warrants, options and units or shares in a mutual fund.

The government claims the plan will cut the taxes paid on capital gains earned from the sale of what is held in an ISIP. Investors will be taxed on the part of capital gains over and above the rate of inflation. Calculations will be made monthly. At the end of the year, the adjusted cost of the stock will be subtracted from the market price of the share with 25 per cent of the difference reported and taxed as capital gain. Capital losses will be treated the same way.

Obviously, the higher the rate of inflation the more ISIPs will help individual investors. Critics also point out that administrative costs could be sky high and that long-term investors might not want to pay tax on accrued gains with today's dollars when they could defer paying until they actually sold the shares, at which time they would pay tax in depreciated dollars.

Keep tuned to developments. ISIPs could, or could not, be great for women trying to get a handle on financial planning.

Other Kinds of Investments

GICs, term deposits, mutual funds, money-market funds, T-Bills, mortgages — there are dozens of ways to invest your money outside the stock or bond market. Make sure you know what you are doing before you put your money anywhere. What kind of a return will you get? How long will the money be locked in? What happens if there is an emergency and you need cash now?

Mortgages

Newspapers run ads daily for mortgages with 12- to 14-per-cent returns. Be wary. We have friends who lost considerable amounts of money in mortgage companies that went into receivership. In at least two cases the companies had been around for quite some time, but somehow things got out of hand and the investors were the ones left with empty pockets.

Some lawyers can help you to find a private mortgage in which to invest.

Remember that mortgage income is interest and is taxable after the first $1,000.

We don't say don't invest in mortgages. We do say watch out and be very sure of what you are doing before you do it!

Most women would rather own one home than a lot of houses. You have to know yourself very well before you risk it. However, we know two women, interior designers, who have bought two houses so far, one at a time, and proceeded to remodel and renovate them before selling them at a substantial profit. And they had all the fun (?) of the fixing up.

Money-market Accounts

Money-market funds are very popular in the United States and exist in a limited way in Canada through AGF, Guardian Capital and Bolton Tremblay investment groups, all of Toronto.

The funds take money from investors to put into short-term treasury bills, bank certificates of deposit and some commercial paper (corporate borrowings). Because the return is invested on a short-term basis only, the return is closely related to current interest rates. During the 1981– 82 boom in such rates, investors did extremely well. Now that the rates are down considerably, the return isn't as good.

Mutual Funds

People who don't have the time, patience or interest to create a portfolio of their own often turn to mutual funds for investment. By putting a certain amount of money into a fund they receive a number of shares or units and know that professional managers are pooling money with cash from other investors and making investments.

Mutual funds deal with bonds, stocks, options and even precious gems. Some have been going for 20 or 30 years and have excellent track records; others are new. The financial media does a review of funds on a periodic basis so readers can compare track records going back several years.

Mutual funds were the thing in the 1960s but dropped drastically in value during the 1970s. Some investors have just now gotten out of their funds after waiting many years to break even.

If you are in the market for a mutual fund, talk to people who specialize in selling them; check out track records yourself; discuss them with people who hold fund units or shares.

Legally, brokers can charge up to 9 per cent commission on the buying of mutual funds. If you put $1,000 into one of these "load" funds, you will find that after commission only $910 of your $1,000 is left to work for you. It can take a long time to make that amount of money back.

However, there are "no-load" funds, which don't charge you a commission either going in or getting out. Look at these funds, too, and decide which kind is for you. If you do decide to invest in a "load" fund, remember commissions are negotiable, so bargain. Sometimes you can save a lot that way.

Ways to Lose Money

When is an investment not an investment? Experts can cite dozens of examples of ways to lose money. The most common are:

- The beloved penny stocks of the Vancouver Stock Exchange players who don't let facts stand in the way of a good rumour. Greed is the motivating factor here; everyone wants something for nothing. What one often gets is nothing for something. If you want to play the pennies, use only money you are prepared to lose. Remember that stock-exchange history is littered with stories of companies that went up and up and up and up and then collapsed into bankruptcy. More than 1,200 companies once listed on Canadian stock exchanges don't exist any longer. All had hopes and dreams and shareholders before they went under.
- Diamonds are not a girl's best friend if she buys the stones at retail prices and then tries to sell them. Usually, such sales bring only wholesale prices and the mark-up on precious gems is colossal. You can unload a diamond, ruby or emerald through auctions, some jewellery stores, dealers or pawn-brokers, but don't expect more than a fraction of what the stone may be worth if it's appraised by a gemologist. The only way some people get what they consider to be the true value of a diamond is if it happens to be lost and was insured for replacement value. To qualify for such insurance, the stone must have been appraised in the proper manner by a certified gemologist.
- There is an old saying that if wishes were horses, beggars would

115

ride. But horses have probably beggared more people than most other so-called "investments." If you have a Kentucky Derby winner you rake in the cash, but there is only one such winner among thousands of horses bought by hopeful owners each year. More than 96 per cent of all race-horse owners are said to lose money. They do help the economy with the money they pour into trainers' fees, vets, jockeys and feed bills, but of the total cost of up to $15,000 a year, only $5,000 can be deducted on your income tax as a loss. That leaves $10,000 a year to come out of your pocket.

- Limited editions can be a snare and a delusion if the only limit is on demand. Remember Canada's famous Olympic coins? All previous issues of such coins took dramatic upturns immediately after they were bought; in Canada we manufactured so many coins that they could have been bought months, even years, after the 1976 Olympics for less than issue price.

- It's easier to make money at a gambling casino than it is on a lottery ticket. Most government lotteries give away less than 55 per cent of their collections in cash prizes, whereas the average gambling casino pays out about 95 per cent of what it takes in to winners.

Collectibles

Collectibles are an emotional investment. People keep trying to justify them after the fact by telling themselves their glass paperweight from the 1902 Canadian National Exhibition is worth a fortune, but unless you find another nut who can't live without a glass paperweight from the 1902 CNE, you won't make any money on it.

You keep reading stories about someone who sold his early Batman comics for thousands of dollars, or the old umbrella jar in the hall that turned out to be Ming Dynasty, but it's like winning lotteries: it always happens to someone else. If you like collecting, fine. Your spoon or coin collection, your dolls or your thimbles can give you a great deal of pleasure. On paper — that is, on your asset sheet — they look like money. All we can say is, don't bank on it.

Collectibles are called "sterile assets." They don't give you any interest (not that kind) and they don't give you a tax shelter. They may accrue in value, but only if you find the right buyer who'll take your hair rings off your hands. True, antiques are worth a lot, especially when you go to buy one. But when you go to sell it, an antique piece

116

of furniture has to be exquisite and in perfect condition; otherwise, it's second-hand sticks.

If you're really interested in collecting and want to get in on crazes at the very beginning, heed the experts who say that the things that "may" be hot in the future are long-playing-record jackets, first-edition paperbacks (you know, the kind you have been donating to garage and church sales for the past 10 years because they were "only paperbacks"), anything to do with Coca Cola (watches, trays, etc.), theatre programs and even the operating instructions for small appliances!

Scripophilia is the name given by contestants in a *London Times* contest to the newest collecting craze in Europe — old stock certificates. There are fewer than 10,000 people presently collecting such certificates in North America and the field is wide open. Rummage sales, old dresser drawers, second-hand shops, even lawyers' offices are ripe for the picking. If you come across any old certificates, ask a stockbroker to find out if the company that issued the certificate is still alive. If it is, the stock may have some value. If it isn't, tell the broker not to throw the certificate away. Stock certificates that predate 1939 are the most valuable, but if you hold onto newer ones long enough, they may bring you in some cash in the future.

Old railway certificates are particularly prized because of the ornate engraving, the bright colours and the lavish decoration. Apparently the fly-by-night companies that sprang up across the country thought that the more ornate the certificate the more prosperous-looking the company. That left a lot of Canadians with worthless stock, the only potential of which is now the actual certificate. Sotheby's have sales of such certificates through their London offices and catalogues are available.

When you next clean out your attic, check for such unlikely finds as a Barbie doll complete with its original packaging. If you find one, your day and your fortune will be made. Barbie, plus package, is literally worth her weight in gold. What anyone would be doing with an unopened doll package we don't know, but look anyway. You never can tell what's stowed away upstairs, downstairs or in the garage.

There's a bi-monthly magazine called *Collectibles Illustrated* for people interested in collecting things. Write: Yankee, Inc., Dublin, New Hampshire, USA 03444.

Keep in mind another one of Paul Dickson's Rules: "Anything billed as 'destined to be a collector's item' won't be," and the Corollary: "Things that aren't, will be."

12

Real Estate

*"Men no longer regard the place where they
live as a home. It is merely a speculation
in real estate."*
PETER McARTHUR

A Home Is Not a House

Men may regard a house as a real-estate speculation; that's their business. It has more mystic overtones to a woman, probably because up until now so few women have been able to become women of property in their own right.

Real Estate

Real estate is an emotional investment. It takes a very different kind of mind and personality to get into real estate in a serious, commercial way than it does to get into the stock market. One house, okay. But trading up from house to house to make a profit is very different, also very time-consuming. You could call it a full-time occupation, even. What we want to talk about is buying your own house.

So let's talk about one house — yours. Our economy has changed so much that couples starting out can no longer simply assume that they will one day own their own homes. One way of getting a leg up on a house is through an RHOSP (see page 69). It used to be that the only way a woman alone could own a house was to inherit it — from a deceased parent or spouse (with the help of mortgage-cancellation insurance). Now women are actively going about the business of buying their own homes. Why not? A house is still a good investment, a hedge against inflation, and there are ways to make the interest on your investment tax deductible.

119

Houses, Condos, and Co-ops

A house is usually a separate unit on its own plot of land, but it could also be a row house, a duplex, a triplex, or a semi-detached. It's your castle, though, yours and the mortgage company's, and you can do anything you want with it in terms of decor and gardening, providing the neighbours don't object and local laws don't forbid it.

A condominium is a unit in what may look like a house or an apartment building or semi-detached or townhouse. You own the unit but not the common areas (halls, recreation areas, both indoors and out, swimming pool, and so on) which are shared by the residents. Like the house, it carries an individual (as opposed to a blanket) mortgage, on which you make regular payments, plus a monthly fee to cover the maintenance costs of the common areas.

A co-op is also a unit with shared spaces, but the owners own the shared spaces as well. You buy a certain number of shares. These entitle you to a unit of a certain size, according to the number of shares you own. If the co-op has a blanket mortgage, it is not as attractive a deal. One of us is in a co-op apartment with individual mortgages. Again, as with the condo, you pay a monthly assessment for upkeep.

Buying a House

Almost everyone wants to own the roof over her head but not everyone can really afford a house, condo, or townhouse. Housing prices fluctuate like everything else in a buy-sell market and you have to choose your time well. Sharp bargaining is acceptable and you can even shop around for a mortgage. It's a little like jumping into a double skipping rope at pepper speed: calculate the risk and keep your balance and you'll be fine.

How Much Will It Cost

Don't even think about buying unless you can afford to put from 10 per cent to 20 per cent of the purchase price into a down payment. Remember that you will also need cash for:

- closing costs
    - the fees paid to your lawyer,
    - the land transfer tax, if applicable,
    - your share of the year's house taxes (if you take possession February 1 you will be responsible for the taxes covering the eleven months of the year you own the house; if the house becomes yours October 1 your share will cover only three months),

120

- the estimated cost of what heating oil is left in the basement tank,
- appliances — if this is your first house you will probably need a stove and refrigerator, and perhaps a washer and dryer, as well as such incidentals as lawn mower, hoses, rakes, other gardening tools, hammer, saw, chisel and a plunger for unplugging drains and toilets,
- moving — your movers will want cash on delivery and if you don't pay you won't get your furniture unloaded,
- necessary renovations.

The costs of owning a home take in a lot more than the mortgage. In addition you have to be prepared for:

- an annual tax bill amounting to several hundreds or even thousands of dollars,
- insurance — both your home and contents should be insured for replacement cost and you should also have liability insurance, which protects you if someone falls down your stairs or slips on your floors and is incapacitated for some time,
- utilities — those hydro, telephone, heating and water bills come along with monotonous regularity and have to be paid if service is to continue,
- repairs — it's only after you live in a house that you find out how many things can, and do, go wrong,
- maintenance — roofs do wear out, wiring needs to be updated, sidewalks can crumble and eavestroughing needs to be replaced. Add some painting, papering and general sprucing up, and even if you do it all yourself, you are talking about what could be considerable amounts of money!

The experts say you shouldn't take on a mortgage if the monthly payments, when added to property taxes, would total more than 30 per cent of your total monthly income. We would go further. Don't commit more than 30 per cent of your net (take-home after deductions) pay to housing, which should include mortgage (principal and interest), taxes, insurance and utilities (hydro, water, telephone).

Deciding To Buy

Take a look at your monthly housing costs now and see if there would be a financial advantage to buying your own home. Have you got enough cash (or CSBs or GICs or RHOSPs easily liquidated into cash) for the down payment and closing costs, plus any appliances you will need? Would your mortgage payments be much higher than the amount you are presently paying in rent? Are you in a rent-controlled apartment where you know what increases will be annually, or in a suite where rent can jump 20 per cent or more without warning? Would it give you a feeling of satisfaction and safety to own your own home?

If the answers to these questions come out in favour of a house, start looking.

Protect Yourself

When you have found a house you are interested in buying, take some steps to protect yourself from yourself:

- Don't sign an ''interim'' agreement to buy unless you realize it isn't ''interim'' at all, but a legally binding contract that becomes valid when you sign it. One out is to include conditional clauses stipulating that the deal hinges on the sale of your home, or on getting acceptable financing or on the approval of your lawyer;
- Have your lawyer check out any and all agreements before you sign and make them conditional on his/her approval;
- Have your lawyer make sure the fences are really on the property line and that there are caveats on neighbouring houses to protect your view but not on the house you are interested in that would prevent future additions;
- Write warranties into the agreement from the builder or seller on the roof, plumbing, wiring, foundation, drainage;
- Admit you don't know what to look for yourself (if you don't) and hire a professional to inspect the house. Look in the Yellow Pages under ''Building Inspection Service'' or ''Inspection Services — Buildings'' for a choice. Check out the companies listed with your local Better Business Bureau and/or your provincial department of consumer affairs. A reputable inspector will charge you between $100 and $200 for an average-size house and will give you a complete report on what he/she finds;
- Know your real-estate agent; his/her personal integrity can mean a lot;
- Find local courses on how to look for, find and buy a house. The Vancouver school board offers eight-week sessions called ''How To Buy A Used House,'' which tell you how to set about finding your dream home and give you information on zoning,

122

structures, foundation, electrical, heating and plumbing systems, the condition of the chimneys and the roof, and so on. Such attention to detail may take the glamour out of house-hunting but it can save you thousands of dollars in the long run and perhaps keep you from making a bad and costly mistake;

- Real estate is not always a clear road to your financial fortune. Remember, rental property has to be looked after, tenants checked, rents collected, repairs made; raw land may or may not go up in value, but while it is just sitting there your money is tied up not earning anything. And real-estate prices can go down just as quickly as they go up.

Getting Your Mortgage

Credit unions, banks and trust companies as well as private individuals lend mortgage money. Today, it is more common than it used to be to have the seller of the house offer to take back a mortgage — literally lend you the money to buy the house, in the form of a mortgage. Sometimes this is an asset, because individuals often charge less than the financial institutions.

A conventional mortgage demands a down payment of 25 per cent of the appraised value of the house with the mortgage lender providing the other 75 per cent. A high-ratio mortgage requires only a 10-per-cent down payment with the mortgage covering 90 per cent, but it must be insured against default by the federal government's Canada Mortgage and Housing Corporation or the Mortgage Insurance Company of Canada.

Try to pay extra if you can. Your aim should be to own 25 per cent of the purchase price of the house. This will affect refinancing, if you come to that. If you do not own 25 per cent of your home when the mortgage comes due, then you must apply to CMHC again.

In some instances the person selling the house may offer to take a second mortgage if a potential buyer can't raise the necessary funds for a down payment. The holder of a first mortgage would have first call on the money if the house had to be sold because payments weren't made. The second mortgage holder would get the next call.

Refinancing

There are a number of reasons to refinance, some of them valid, some of them sad, some of them frivolous. If you have remodelled your kitchen or added a swimming pool or a family room, thereby increasing the value of the house, you might want to refinance after re-assessing

123

the house. You take out a new mortgage, pay off the old one and hope you have some money left over to invest. Be sure that you can carry the new load and that your investment makes it worth while.

We know a single woman who lost her house when her mortgage came due and the interest rates were so high she couldn't keep up her payments. Such refinancing, through no fault of yours, can be very painful. Our friend had to sell her house for less than she paid for it in order to pay off her intolerable mortgage. It literally is unbearable when interest rates are unbearable.

Once your home is paid for (it happens), you might think about remortgaging it in order to gain some extra cash for investment purposes. This way the interest you pay on the mortgage would be tax deductible. This holds true, however, only if you conform to certain provisos. You have to prove what you're doing with the money. Check with an accountant or a tax expert.

In days of high interest it's often better to use your house to buy a car than to use the finance company. You can refinance the house and get a lower interest rate, calculated semi-annually in advance, than you can get from the finance company, which will charge higher interest, subject to possible change. Or it might be worthwhile to consider a second mortgage, sometimes available at the same rate of interest as the first one. Remember, however, to count the cost of the fees involved. There's no such thing as a free lunch.

Renegotiating Your Mortgage

Credit unions, banks and trust companies are being flooded with requests now to renegotiate mortgages granted in the high-interest days of 1981 and 1982. If you were smart enough to have a clause inserted in your mortgage giving you the right to renegotiate during the term of the mortgage, congratulations. If you weren't, take heart, it can be done. Friends of ours were told verbally, but not in writing, that their 19.5 per cent mortgage could be renegotiated if rates went down and if they paid a penalty of three months' interest. Months later when they applied, the trust company demanded a payment of 10 months' interest. They fought the penalty through their provincial department of consumer affairs and took their complaint to the trust company's head office. To facilitate matters they did pay the 10 months' penalty but within two weeks of applying to head office for relief they had a cheque in their mailbox for the extra seven months' interest. They found it was important to keep their cool, check their facts, and approach the problem realistically.

124

- Shop around for a mortgage. Rates may vary by as much as half or three-quarters of a percentage point from institution to institution;
- Put down as much as you can on the house. The higher the down payment the less you have to pay in interest over the coming years. Work it out for yourself. You may be stunned to find you will actually fork out many times the value of the mortgage. There has never been a better argument for coming up with the largest down payment you possibly can.
- If you can afford to, take a shorter amortization (the number of years over which the mortgage will be paid off) than the 25 years normally offered. The longer the amortization the lower the monthly payments but the higher the amount paid in interest. Cutting the amortization period from 25 to 15 years can reduce the total cost of the house by thousands and thousands of dollars.
- Look for an "open" mortgage that allows you to repay some of the debt without having to fork out for heavy penalty payments. With a "closed" mortgage such repayments are either not permissible or cost several months' extra interest.
- Think seriously about the term of your mortgage — the length of time it would be in effect. Mortgages are offered in terms lasting from six months to five years and rates vary considerably depending on which you choose. One disadvantage to taking a short-term mortgage — six months or a year — is that it costs money in fees every time you renew. As a general rule, if you think interest rates are going up, take the longest-term mortgage you can find; if you think interest is on its way down, try for a short-term mortgage with the thought of lower rates at renewal time. In all cases, know how and when you can pay off your mortgage, renegotiate terms, or make extra payments to lower the principal.

Joint Ownership

Although we seem to have been aiming much of the discussion here at single women, many in the market for the first time for their own homes, we haven't forgotten married women. We recommend joint ownership of the home you share with your spouse. It's another case of yours, mine, ours where ours, as usual, speaks of faith and trust. However, if faith and trust are eroded, it's harder to get a house away from you that's in both your names. In the event of the spouse's death, property transfer is much simpler because the mate's name is already on the title.

Second Homes

There are many reasons for women to own second homes. In the case of married couples, the second home, whether it's a summer cottage, a ski chalet, or a shack on some dream property in the Gulf Islands (we know several couples with such properties), can be entirely the property of the wife. It used to be that you could make one home the principal residence of one spouse, the other the principal residence of the other, with resulting tax breaks on the sale of either house. That loophole was blocked in the 1983 budget, but there are women who could still prove that such buildings are invaluable for their own purposes: writers, potters, photographers, musicians, weavers, artists, singers. Women with careers or about-to-be-careers welcome the facilities of a second residence as hide-away and studio. If the house is close enough to the first one, it can be used on a regular enough basis to justify the expenses.

The Summer Cottage

Anyone who saw the film or play *On Golden Pond* needs no statement from us about the cumulative effect on the emotions and the psyche of owning your own summer place that you go back to year after year after year. One of us had a summer home in the Whiteshell in Manitoba and the children miss that place more than any home we lived in in Winnipeg. It was a constant, while the other houses changed over the years.

That cottage, shared with parents who owned it, was sold for a dollar to one of us — one of the best deals ever transacted! And more common than you might think. If you're lucky enough to fall heir to such a real-estate bargain then you have merely the problem of upkeep and maintenance of your second property to tend to with none of the burden of paying for it. But there are ways to manage ownership of a second property, once you have decided on its desirability.

Retirement Homes

For those fortunate enough to be hoping for company in their retirement, couples who have stood the tests of temptation and time and survived, a retirement home of one's own makes a lot of sense. It could be the summer cottage, winterized — and we know several

126

couples who have been working toward that. It could also be a piece of land with a shack, as we mentioned, ideal now for get-away-from-it-all summer vacations, but held with an eye to developing it as a permanent home on retirement.

If a man (or woman) is handy, a house can be built as a shell. Then the finishing of it becomes the retirement project, more demanding than any day job ever was and very satisfying. This kind of enterprise solves two of the problems of retirement: what to do with your time, and how to afford what you want on a fixed income. Doing it yourself, as you know, saves a pile of money.

Not an Impossible Dream

You may think of a second home as an impossible dream, but it need not be. It's still possible to find bargains in rural areas, much cheaper than houses in our big cities. Purchased with an eye to long-range holding, such a bargain can become a stabilizing factor in your life, not only emotionally but even, eventually, financially. All you need is foresight.

Some women, and couples, too, who find that their city home is too big as the children peel off and go their own ways, use the first home to finance the second one. That is, they usually trade down for a smaller property in the city, or even go into an apartment. Then they use the money they have released from the sale to pay for the second property.

Rental Property

If you don't plan to use the second property for some time, that is, until you retire, and it's too far away to be easily accessible to you where you live and work, then you can rent it. Your rent then helps to pay for the mortgage payments you're making. And if you make any improvements on the property while you are renting it, what you spend is deductible from your income tax because it is money spent to enhance your income. That's nice.

We know some city people who have bought small working farms as their second homes and they get good tax breaks for that, because the federal government smiles on farmers. The farm owners can lease the farm to tenant farmers who live in the house on the property. Or they can lease some of the land to neighbouring farmers who want extra crop land. Or they can raise cattle (we know one couple who does this) and hire someone to do the daily chores while they come and work and enjoy on the weekends. Or they can grow trees. The

127

government subsidizes such a project, offering seedlings at low prices to encourage replanting of trees on land that is otherwise unoccupied. And all these ploys earn good tax deductions, enabling the possession and payments for a property destined to be a retirement paradise. Think about it.

Shopping for a House

First or second home, you have to be careful when you're shopping for a house. You may fall in love with a flowering plum tree in the front garden, but be sure the plumbing works, too. Take an architect or an engineer with you and get a realistic assessment of the house. And re-read *Mr. Blandings Builds His Dream House* so you can laugh about the mistakes you'll cry about if you make them.

Two Rules

If we had to sum up all our cautionary statements without discouraging you too much, we would go back to our tired tried-but-true imperative: shop around. Ask questions. Talk. And be assured that almost everything can be negotiated. Lots of people buy decorating — that's why you paint and spruce up before you try to sell your place.

We know someone who had to leave the stuff in her front hall for the buyers. It was what used to be called a vestibule. It had a black bench to sit on while putting on boots, a black wrought-iron candle sconce on the white-painted wall with a white candle in it, a red-and-white-striped awning on the inside of the window and a radiator painted red. Everything stayed, including the radiator!

The point is, things can be negotiated. We have friends in Bermuda who got two watchdogs with the house they bought.

The other point, more serious, is that you should get everything in writing. People make promises they either forget or never intended to keep. If they say they'll leave the chandelier in the dining room, get it in writing. If they say they'll fix the garage door, get it in writing. Don't rely on goodwill or faulty memories. Spell it all out when you make your offer — in writing!

If at First You Don't Succeed

If your first offer or bid on a house is turned down, make another offer. More likely, you will receive a counter-offer. Generally speaking, North Americans don't bargain when they shop. But this statement does not apply to house-buying. You bargain a lot when you buy a house, until you come upon a price that is mutually agreeable.

Then you make a deposit, a chunk of money to be held as evidence of good faith and intent, to be applied to the purchase price when all systems are go and the rest of the money is due, too.

Selling a House

We've already dropped a hint or two that you can use when you are selling your house. Painting and fixing things is essential. You want to put on your best appearance. As we said, some people buy decorating. But we know a woman who swears she sold her house because she was baking bread when the people who turned out to be the buyers came for an inspection. Somethin' lovin' from the oven sold that house!

It never hurts to be friendly. We have sold two properties by inviting the people to stay and have a drink on their second or third inspection. This way you can chat about the neighbourhood, the schools, the shopping and so on. After all, you're selling a place to live, not just a heap of bricks and mortar. Do your haggling through the real-estate agent — and we recommend using one rather than trying to sell the house yourself.

Growing Market

We are told that the single woman is the fastest growing market for real estate today, and her goal is not a quick return on her dollars. She wants a home of her own, a roof she can call hers, shelter and security, to say nothing of the satisfaction of knowing that she's buying it all by herself. No help wanted.

13

Children and Money

"The young are improvident — not having yet learned how hard to come by money is and of how little account are other things."
MARGARET WIDDEMER

It's still easier to talk to your kids about money than about sex, but not much. With both subjects, there's a lot of emotion involved. It's all in your attitude, and you can be sure that, just as your attitude to sex is going to be apparent to your children even if you don't say a word, so is your attitude to money. As a loving parent, you want to guide your children in money matters and help them develop an understanding of how money works and how to become wise consumers. If only someone had told you!

Money is like what George Bernard Shaw said youth was: wasted on the young. But the attitudes they develop in youth are going to last them a lifetime. For their sakes, help them to feel good about money, and about themselves in relation to money. Help them not to feel envy or greed; help them to be generous; help them not to be too chintzy or tight; help them to enjoy money without being fearful and to use it always as merely one of the tools of living and not as an end in itself.

Money is one of the facts of life children can learn early. One of the basic facts is that you can't have everything you want. You have to choose, you have to make decisions, you have to learn how to put off present indulgences for future satisfaction. Money, you see, can become a building block of character, if you let it.

As in every other area of human learning, one learns a great deal oneself when one attempts to teach others. If you didn't know them before, you will discover things about money when you start teaching

131

your children about it. Of course, they learn a lot about how you feel before you ever open your mouth. They see what you're doing. They see whether you buy on impulse or whether you have a plan for spending. They see whether you follow your plan, whether you plan ahead for special needs or extra treats, or whether you live from one day to the next, buying according to what's in your purse and how you feel. They see whether you comparison shop, whether you buy no-frills, generic labels, whether you buy the most expensive brands, whether you decide each case, can or package on its own merit and price. They learn far more from on-the-spot observation like this than they ever do from those horrible homey lectures you may have suffered through when you were a kid.

Learning What Money Is For

Remember the line, "You young people today expect to be rewarded for being good. When I was your age I was good for nothing." Lectures like that have no effect whatsoever. Still, you want to teach your children respect for money. To do that, they have to have money they can count on, not an income that is subject to your whims or their good behaviour or chores. That's what an allowance is for — a base sum, paid on a regular basis (once a week, twice a month, monthly, depending on the age and maturity of the child) that your son or daughter can plan with. This should not be dependent on behaviour. Extra money can be earned for chores, with an agreed-upon price. We know one family who has a price list of chores attached by magnets to the refrigerator door (every family's bulletin board — whatever did they do in the days of ice boxes?). When a kid in that family wants extra money, he looks up the list and negotiates — and performs!

Just as children learn and grow in other areas, so they develop their expertise and sophistication by handling money. They learn how to:

- manage an allowance
- earn money
- plan ahead
- save for the future — usually for something concrete, like a new bicycle, camera or stereo equipment
- borrow and lend money — negotiate deals, usually beginning with mother
- buy presents (Christmas and birthdays for the family, later for girlfriends or boyfriends)
- shop around

132

- eventually learn the family money plan and help implement it
- make up a weekly grocery list (that involves some meal planning)
- shop for food and other needs
- be in on family discussions, maybe even help shop for major purchases

We began our meal-planning, shopping and cooking lessons simultaneously when our daughters had had an initiation to home economics (or whatever schools call it now — consumer training?). During their summer vacations, they were required to plan a couple of weeks' menus, shop for them and then prepare the meals according to their plan. Result: a holiday for mother! Plus some valuable hands-on training.

One of our daughters used to play store before she could see the top of a till. She used to "make change," which meant stirring the pasteboard coins she had in a pot on her make-believe store counter. Money is a toy to children. They see you put coins in a parking meter, for which you get nothing, coins in a pay phone, for which you get to talk (and you can do that for nothing at home), in a Coke machine, for which you get a bottle of something good to drink — now, that's more like it! And coins in another machine that gives you peanuts or a chocolate bar or whatever. When you think of how quickly they progress to the point where they want cross-country skis and all the latest hit recordings and Calvin Klein jeans and Sony Walkmans and ten-speed bicycles and cars — it's depressing.

Use Money Wisely

So help them learn how to use money wisely. Explain as you go along. Give them the opportunity to shop with you, to make choices, even bad ones, according to your view. They learn by their own mistakes, just as you learn by yours. Make sure you teach them as soon as possible that hard lesson you have learned about putting aside something for savings first. Be sure they have the opportunity to give to others, too, to charity or church or synagogue, to community service of some kind, so that they know their private responsibility for public well-being. Teach them how to be generous, to buy gifts for family and friends at special times. Make sure they understand the limits of your money so they do not develop unreal expectations. A lot of parents sacrifice their own desires to satisfy their children beyond their means. Take into account your own standards of living, and make sure your children understand them.

133

We can still remember the surprised look of understanding when one of our daughters complained of having to wear her school tunic to school all the time instead of just on gym days. We explained that it was cheaper for her to do so, that we didn't have to buy her as many clothes that way. (Nowadays, of course, all kids wear jeans to school.) After that, she never complained.

Children's Attitudes to Money

You can check out any number of books on child development to find out what your child is capable of understanding about money and its uses at a given age, and the extent to which he/she needs guidance. In addition to whatever normal development takes place, there are individual characteristics that emerge. You'll find children in the same family with very different attitudes to money: one is a born miser and has to be coaxed to spend money; another is a spendthrift and treats himself and his friends as if money were water running through his hands; another likes to save but for a purpose, and shops carefully, but when he decides to spend, he does so thoroughly. One of our children is a Libra, the scales, and weighs every purchase as carefully as if he were weighing it on those scales of his. He's our best shopper and has saved us a lot of money by making some of our major purchases (like stereo components) for us. If you have a born shopper on your hands, be grateful.

At whatever stage of maturity and financial experience your child is, you will continually be astonished at the amount of money he/she needs. It doesn't help much to compare with other parents how they handle their children's allowances because you'll find that everyone has a different attitude and handles money differently. Besides, only you know how much you can afford. Better to have your son or daughter keep a record of how much money he/she spends over two or three weeks — like those diet diaries when you have to record every mouthful you take in. Use a chart — and introduce your children to the wonderful world of lists! Call it the "Easy Come, Easy Go Chart." Your purpose, of course, is to show them how easily it leaves the pocket and how hard it is to come by.

Easy Come, Easy Go Chart

	Week One Planned/Spent	Week Two Planned/Spent	Week Three Planned/Spent
Regular expenses:			
Savings			
Church/ Community			
Transportation			
Club dues (Cubs, Brownies, etc.)			
Lunches			
Discretionary expenses:			
Snacks			
Magazines			
Books			
Movies			
Entertainment			
Cosmetics			
Toiletries			
Hobbies/ Sports			
Clothes			
Other			
TOTALS			

The regular or fixed expenses, of course, can't be changed and have to be allowed for. The unplanned, discretionary expenses are irregular and vary with the individual. Most of them come under the heading of "fun" and can be cut down if the totals are too high. Take a look at the planned amount and the amount actually spent, and help your child to come to a fair amount of money he/she can manage on without being a social outcast, a miser, a spendthrift, an ungrateful child or your personal ticket to debtors' prison.

Money and Character

You already know what it's like. It takes a lot of self-control to stay within a budget. No one can be perfect all the time. Be as kind to your children as you are to yourself and forgive them if they slip once in a while.

In spite of the unemployment figures, most kids manage to earn extra money, by baby-sitting, mowing lawns, shovelling snow, delivering newspapers, and even catering. The tougher times are for you, the more you find your children can manage. It's one of the ironies of life, in fact, that kids who have to work a little, scrimp a bit and save a lot for their future (read education) often end up the most goal-oriented, the least likely to drop out of school or college because they're not sure what they want to do with their lives. If they've had to put up the money for it, they already know what they want and they don't intend to blow it.

We have a friend whose mother was a widow and raised him during the Depression. She taught him something it might be useful for you to remember and tell your children. "If you can't afford something, don't buy it and don't settle for less. When you have to spend money, buy the best you can afford." We think that's what we mean when we say: don't be chintzy.

It's a question of priorities again, and perhaps also of definition. You can teach your children to be frugal without being chintzy. You can teach them to know value when they see it and not to throw good money away on cheap returns. Teach them, if you can, what our mothers taught us: how to make one dollar do the work of two, and look like five.

Another rule your children should learn: don't bum, leech, cadge, poach, mulch or mooch. People who smoke O.P.'s, who are constantly out-fumbled for a cheque, who never get their hands out of their pockets fast enough, are soon identified. You don't want either you or your children to bear the label.

As for stealing, this is a book about money, not morals. There's stealing and stealing, and your children learn about that, too, before you say a word. If you never mention a mistake in your favour at the check-out counter, if you pad an expense account or fudge your income-tax statements, your kids will get the idea soon enough how you feel about the eighth commandment. Stealing money from your purse or from a neighbour's kid or from school funds — everyone knows the rules about that, and you can deal with those early in your child's

136

life, and promptly when the incident occurs. Just make sure she is old enough to understand the difference between mine-theirs, that she has enough money of her own for her necessities, that stealing doesn't seem like a Robin-Hood thing to do, that she hasn't been egged on to do it by a friend, and that she is getting enough attention and TLC from her family.

Envy is something else. One of us had a mother who taught us not to envy. "When you see a friend with a dress or a possession you admire," she used to say, "say so. That way you have *given* your friend something, and you don't have to take anything away by envy." In other words, expose it to the air; give it away. Be realistic. All these attitudes are useful for grownups as well as for children.

Above all, teach your children to plan for the future. We have read that the present generation of teenagers is the first since World War Two who cannot hope to better their parents' position. There are young people today who can never hope to own their own home, who will put off having children because they are so expensive to raise, who will dread their retirement because they'll never be able to afford it. None of us can afford to coast on the assumptions of the past. It's a different world, and the future is not what it used to be.

Still, it's worth hanging around to see what it's going to be like. Just because it's not going to be like the past is nothing to worry about. How could it be? We're different from what we were. And our children are different again. They know more about sex than we ever did. Pretty soon they're going to start telling us about money, too.

14

Estate Planning and Property Settlement

"If you were going away on a trip and leaving children behind, you'd leave instructions for the baby-sitter, wouldn't you?"
BETTY JANE WYLIE

Attitudes to Wills

Damon Runyon didn't like to go too close to jails because, as he said, "peepings may be catching." People feel that way about wills. They figure the farther they stay away from them, the less will be their need for them. Not so.

But it's a reverse-umbrella syndrome. You know perfectly well that if you take an umbrella with you it won't rain. People have the idea reversed when it comes to making a will and planning for a future in which they do not exist. If they don't do it, they think, they won't die. No one will notice them because they haven't tempted fate or made any waves, so they can slip through life undetected. Perhaps this attitude is the reason that 70 per cent of men die without a will.

We have a double-bladed axe to grind. One: those of you who are married have to make sure your husbands have wills, and that you're in them. Two: you should have a will as well.

Do Your Will Now

A lot of women put off having a will drawn up because they "haven't anything to leave to anyone, anyway." Face it, it depresses you. Forget the excuses. Do your will now. If you don't, your estate passes to beneficiaries according to the laws of the province or the territory in which you live, in amounts and percentages that may not reflect what you really want to happen with your money and possessions.

139

People who die without wills leave behind added expense, inconvenience and often ill-feelings in the settlement of their estates. If you make out a will, your survivors will know how you wanted things done and you will have made things as easy as possible for them.

Married women, particularly those with small children, should make sure that their husbands have their wills in order.

No Will

Here's what happens to the estate when someone dies without a will:

1. *If you leave a spouse, no children, no issue:*
a. your estate goes to your spouse in all provinces except Quebec;
b. in *Quebec* it goes to the spouse only if you die with no living children, parents, brothers, sisters, nephews or nieces.
c. In *Quebec*, if you die without a will leaving a spouse, no children but parents, or no children, no parents, but brothers and sisters: one-half goes to your spouse, the other half to father and mother or survivor and if none survive, to brothers and sisters.
d. Again in *Quebec,* if you die without a will, leaving a spouse and no children, but a father, mother, brothers, sisters: one-third goes to the spouse, one-third to the father and mother or survivor and one-third to brothers and sisters.

---

2. *If you leave a spouse, one child or issue:*
a. a certain amount of money from the estate goes to the spouse, the rest is split 50-50 between spouse and child. In *British Columbia* the first $20,000 goes to the spouse; in *Alberta* and *Saskatchewan,* $40,000; *Manitoba* and *Nova Scotia,* $50,000; *Ontario,** $75,000. In *New Brunswick* the personal chattels go to the spouse, the rest is evenly divided, spouse and child.
b. in *Prince Edward Island* and *Newfoundland* the estate goes half to the spouse, half to the child.
c. in *Quebec* the division is one-third to the spouse, two-thirds to the child.

---

3. *If you die with no will and leave no spouse, but a child or children:* in all provinces the estate goes to the child or is divided equally among the children. In all provinces but *Quebec*, the children of a dead child (grandchildren) get the parent's share.

---

*In Ontario the children of a deceased child (grandchildren) get their parents' share.

4. *If you die without a will, leaving a spouse and two or more children or issue:*

a. the spouse gets a specific amount from the estate, and the remainder is divided, one-third to spouse, two-thirds to be divided equally among the children. This applies in *British Columbia* where the spouse gets the first $20,000, *Alberta* and *Saskatchewan* $40,000 and Ontario, $75,000. In *New Brunswick* the spouse gets the personal chattels before the one-third, two-thirds split.

b. the spouse gets a specific amount of the estate and the remainder is divided with half going to the spouse, half to be divided equally among the children. This applies in *Manitoba* and *Nova Scotia* where the spouse gets the first $50,000.

c. In *Quebec, Prince Edward Island* and *Newfoundland,* the estate is split, one-third to the spouse, two-thirds divided equally among the children.

In all provinces the children of a deceased child (grandchildren) take the child's share.

---

5. *If you die without a will, leaving no spouse, children or issue, your estate goes to:*

a. in *all provinces except Quebec,* to your father and mother; if neither survives, to your brothers and sisters, with children of dead siblings taking their parent's share; if none survives, to nieces and nephews, and if none survives to next of kin.

---

6. *If you die without a will and leave no lawful heirs: your estate will go to*

a. in all provinces your estate will go to "the Crown."

b. In *Alberta* the estate also goes to "the Crown" with provision for the income to be distributed to the universities in the province.

Note that the above information is as current as possible. Naturally, there are other aspects that are not included in some of the divisions. For example, if a spouse dies in British Columbia with no will but leaves a mate and child or children, his/her survivor gets the first $20,000 of the estate and the household furniture and life interest in the family home.

In Quebec, if the marriage took place under what is known as the legal regime of Partnership of Acquests or Community of Property, there are other options for survivors. And in Nova Scotia a spouse may elect to take the family home and contents instead of the first $50,000 of the estate to which he/she is entitled.

141

Check with your own provincial or territorial government to get up-to-date information.

Who Can Make a Will

Anyone who is considered to be mentally competent and of legal age should have his or her own will. It can be changed or cancelled at any time simply by drawing up a new one and revoking the previous one or destroying the original document. If you want to make a simple change in your will, you can add a codicil. A codicil merely amends the will, making a whole new document unnecessary.

Wills for Singles are Important

We know we've said it already but we'll say it again. It is important for everyone to have a will. So you aren't married and/or have no children, siblings, nieces, nephews. You still have friends or favourite charities that you might want to have your estate earmarked for.

Wouldn't you rather that what you had saved and set aside went to someone or something of your choice rather than to "the Crown"? Most people would. It's nice to think of your household goods and possessions being of use to someone else, your money or other investments adding to a good cause.

If education is your delight, you can donate the money for a scholarship in your name to a trade school, community college or university; if heart problems have plagued your family, the Heart Foundation would be overjoyed with a bequest; if civic affairs are your interest, see if there is a foundation in your area that makes money available to local programs.

A Trust Company As Executor

If you are thinking of naming a trust company as your executor, ask for details. Usually the company will provide someone to help you with your will, to discuss any problems and to seal any loopholes. Much of the service is free; the company gets its money as it administers the estate.

Irrevocable Trust

There is one kind of trust fund that can be set up that has a limited but useful aspect. An irrevocable trust is one, obviously, that cannot be revoked; it also does not allow access to the money by the person for whom the money is being administered. This can be a protection for a senile parent or a mentally handicapped person who cannot handle financial matters.

Name A Guardian

If you have children who are minors, be sure to write into your will the name of a guardian who will care for them until they can look after themselves. Also be sure to clear it with the guardian you have in mind, and to discuss it with the children. It could lead to an odd conversation: "I don't like Aunt Soanso's chocolate cake"; "Will we have to take baths every night?"; "Can we stay up to watch the late show?"; "What kind of car do they drive?" Children are very literal-minded and expect you to die once you have made the proper arrangements. Do your best to disappoint them.

What Does An Executor Do

The executor named in your will has certain duties to perform on your behalf:

- arrange for probate of the will;
- pay legacies, debts, taxes and death duties if any;
- keep a complete accounting;
- prepare a statement of assets and liabilities;
- convert investments to cash if need be to pay the bills;
- advertise for creditors;
- redirect mail;
- notify brokers, bankers and insurance agents of death;
- notify beneficiaries;
- ensure that your wishes are carried out;
- value assets if necessary;
- complete life insurance claims and collect the money.

If you leave everything as complete as you can, the executor's work will be easier and your beneficiaries will get their bequests more quickly.

What Constitutes A Legal Will

Your will is legal in all provinces if it is drawn up properly and signed by you at the bottom in the presence of witnesses who also have to sign it in your presence.

Some provinces also accept a holograph will — one you have written in longhand and signed. No witnesses are needed.

Quebec also accepts a will "passed" before a notary as long as he holds the original in safekeeping.

143

Before You Start

Even before you approach your lawyer to have him/her draw up your will, you will need:

- a net-worth statement (remember we did that in chapter one);
- agreement from the person/s you want to be executor/s;
- agreement from those you would name as guardians for your children (one woman we know said that the hardest part of getting such agreement was having to promise to act as guardian for the other couple's children in turn);
- some idea of whom you want to inherit what.

The Nitty-Gritty

Now, the hard part. Write down what you want to happen to your possessions and investments. Be sure to include:

- specific cash bequests to members of your family. You should spell out the amounts, the timing and any special circumstances;
- specific cash bequests to friends, charities, educational institutions or foundations. Include names and amounts;
- specific bequests other than money or investments: antiques, jewellery, art, books, collections;
- disposal of your car, furniture, summer cottage, pets and personal belongings;
- funeral directions;
- anything else you can think of that would be pertinent.

Safeguards

There are some things you might consider before making your will:

- By naming a specific beneficiary for your pension plans, you can ensure that the money will be rolled into his/her RRSP or other plan, thus avoiding tax in the year of your death;
- Mortgages become due and payable on the death of the mortgagee. Buy whole-life or term insurance specifically to pay off the mortgage so that your family doesn't have to come up with the money to pay it off or have to renegotiate when under stress;
- Quebec still levies succession duties, which amount to as much as almost 30 per cent of the taxable part of any estate. If you live there, you can have someone else buy a policy on your life, pay the premiums and then automatically get the proceeds

144

of the policy on your death. This money is not taxable because it is not part of your estate;

- Capital gains or losses are calculated on your investment portfolio as of the day of your death. Nothing has to be paid if you leave the holdings to your spouse, but if you plan to leave them to someone else make sure there is enough cash in the bequest to handle any payments due on recent transactions.

Memorial Societies

If you feel as strongly as some 150,000 Canadians already do, you may want to join a memorial society and specify the kind of funeral arrangements you want for your last farewell. Planning ahead like this doesn't appeal to some people, who fear that, if they do, the worst will happen right away. The worst always happens, face it, but you may save your survivors some pain and some money by making some of their decisions for them in advance. Few people are capable of clear thinking immediately after the death of a loved one, and most of them, in a misdirected rush of love and generosity, tend to overdo the send-off. There are 27 memorial societies in Canada (in every province except Prince Edward Island). They are non-profit and non-denominational. For a nominal fee you can join, investigate the participating funeral facilities and choose a simple arrangement for yourself that won't break your family.

Spare Parts

While you're at it, you might give a thought to the usable bits and pieces you're leaving behind, that is, the usable spare parts of your body. We're not being morbid; far from it. We do not agree with Shakespeare who said, "Oh hell! to choose love by another's eye." It might be kind of fun.

Quite a lot of a human being can be recycled now: kidneys, bones and joints, bone marrow, corneas, brain, heart, lungs, liver, intestines (for research), pancreas, temporal bones (they're in the ear) and pituitary gland. These are 12 parts that are utilized now in the province of Ontario. There are 25 in the United States. Plus skin for burn victims, and we have read of hospitals that use leftover placentas, but you don't have to die to give that away.

Unfortunately, there is no federal legislation that provides jurisdiction for this kind of legacy. You will have to check with your own government to see what's going on. In Ontario, the coroners' office

145

directs the allocation of spare parts, under the Human Tissue Gift Act. In other provinces, the ministry of health usually handles the traffic.

There's a useful anatomical donor card you can use for a model in Leonard Knott's book, *Before You Die*. It's in the appendix — and we refrain from obvious comment.

Matrimonial Property Laws

You may be happily married, you may be engaged and just about to take the big step, or divorce may be rearing its ugly head in your direction — in all cases you should be aware of what will happen if your marriage breaks up. New statistics show that about 40 per cent of this year's marriages will end in divorce, so be prepared and get your affairs in order, just in case.

Matrimonial property laws have come a long way in a short time but many women feel there is still much to be done. In recent years all the provinces and the Yukon have passed legislation providing for the equal sharing of at least some of the spouse's assets on separation or divorce.

But in a paper called "Outline of Matrimonial Property Laws in Canada," Louise Dulude notes that:

> Ontario, British Columbia, Alberta, Prince Edward Island and the Yukon only provide for sharing of the assets of the spouses when the marriage ends in separation or divorce. As a result, widows may end up with a smaller share of the family assets than their divorced or separated counterparts.
>
> - Only Manitoba and Saskatchewan (and possibly Alberta) provide equal sharing of the spouses' most important assets at the end of a marriage. Quebec does not include rights to a future pension* in its sharable property, while most other provinces exclude both pension rights and business or savings property of all kinds.
>
> - the laws of all the provinces and territories except Quebec give too much weight to judicial discretion. As British jurist Olive Stone wrote, judges who are given very broad powers tend to

*When Ms. Dulude discusses "future pensions," she says she means those acquired through employer-sponsored pension plans. "Credits earned under the Canada Pension Plan or the Quebec Pension Plan are held individually by each spouse during the marriage, but will be divided between them after divorce if either applies for splitting within three years of the final decree dissolving their union."

revert to the discredited "one-third rule," which comes from the old Ecclesiastical Courts' presumption that a woman was worth half as much as a man. This is already becoming evident in many Canadian judgments.

British Columbia and possibly Manitoba are exceptions to her statements, as both list employer-sponsored pension plan credits now as family assets.

The chart in the appendix will show you how your province or territory stacks up when it comes to property division at the time of a divorce.

Added Information

In almost all cases where the courts have the discretion to vary sharing of assets there is a long list of criteria that must be taken into consideration. Some provinces list only a few, others have as many as 20 that must be considered before a decision is to be made. In almost all cases, the care of children and housework is included as a contribution to marriage.

Marriage Contracts

As you can see from the tables in the Appendix, people can opt out of the sharing provisions in the provinces and territories by signing marriage contracts or other formal agreements.

Recently, we've met four women from different parts of the country who opted out without understanding what they were doing and who are now suffering the consequences. Just so you or someone in your family doesn't fall into the same trap, take warning:

All four were in troubled marriages. Two knew about the trouble, two didn't. The husbands asked their wives to sign marriage contracts long after their weddings (five to 22 years later), saying they had had the contracts drawn up for "business" or "tax" purposes. All of the wives willingly signed. The two who knew their marriages were shaky said they signed in the hope the contracts would stabilize the situation; the other two signed because they were asked to and were accustomed to doing what their husbands wanted them to do.

Within two years, all four marriages ended, and the women found that they had done themselves out of what they might have had in the way of settlements. They had, in fact, signed most of their rights away.

In all cases the family lawyers drew up the contracts and the women thought the lawyers would protect their interests. In all cases they were

147

wrong. The moral, sad to say, is don't trust your family lawyer.

If your husband wants a post-nuptial marriage contract, insist on your own legal advice. If you can't afford a lawyer, try legal aid; if you don't know one, there is probably a lawyer referral system in your area that can help. Lawyers charge a minimum amount ($1 to $20 for the first half-hour) for a first visit and one trip may be all you need. Even if you have to pay legal fees, it is well worth your while to make sure your rights are protected and that on separation or divorce you won't find you have signed away what was rightfully yours.

Horror stories abound. We know a divorcée whose ex promised her the summer cottage, worth about $25,000. Now he wants to sell it to buy an LTD. She's trying to sock some money away for her retirement in nine years, and could surely use that 25 grand. But she doesn't have anything in writing.

A friend of ours was at a party recently and realized, at about the same time that her husband did, that of all the couples in the room, many of them with children, they were the only ones who were legally married. Furthermore, when she brought up this remarkable fact, the co-vivant women said they were much more protected than most married women because they all had contracts. You might check out Lyn Fels' book on living together (see Additional Reading) and learn the hard facts about such protection.

You can't afford to be dewy-eyed any more. Neither marriages nor star-crossed love affairs are made in heaven. Lawyers' offices may seem cold places to keep a love warm and alive, but they — at least the arrangements you make in them — will keep you warm even if the sheets on the other side of your bed are cold.

We wish we could say something more romantic than that. All we can say is be careful.

15

Record Keeping and Income Tax

*"Nobody was ever meant
To remember or invent
What he did with every cent."*
ROBERT FROST

File It Away

Years ago we knew a housewife with her own filing cabinet. She knew
where everything was, and what's more, could find it, even her sewing
patterns. We were impressed. One of our first filing cabinets was a
Carnation milk-tin carton. It was exactly the width of an 8 1/2" by 11"
manila file-folder. All our recipes and decorating ideas were filed in
it. But there's more to filing than recipes and household ideas.

Even women who pay the household accounts often don't control
the filing system, don't know how the family business really operates
— and we don't necessarily mean the store downtown, but just the
functioning of the family. You need not only a safe place for the
guarantees on appliances, the copies of your credit and charge cards,
the records of your house insurance and municipal tax payments, but
also an easy access to your children's birth certificates, your passports,
your adoption or divorce papers or citizenship papers, if that's applicable, your medical and eyeglass prescriptions. We could go on and
on. And we have, under separate cover (see bibliography).

Then, of course, as you get into the stock market, you need investment files. Although you can keep your record of transactions at
home, it's a good idea to keep your stock certificates, bonds, and so
on in a safety-deposit box, with a record of what's in there stored in
your filing cabinet at home. Don't put your will in the safety-deposit

149

box, though. The box will be sealed for a time after your death and the will required sooner than the box may be opened.

Your insurance policies should be on file, too, as well as information regarding your RSPs and pension plans. We can't tell you how good you'll feel when you have a retrieval system that works. When you want to check something and you can put your hands on the essential information instantly, it gives you a lovely feeling of power — not a bad thing for a so-called helpless woman. In fact, most husbands should be so organized — most men, too.

We know a woman whose husband owned a lucrative little hobby-and-craft store. He died suddenly and our friend was advised to sell the store. She couldn't, at least not right away. His filing system consisted of scraps of paper, notes and reminders pinned to a large bulletin board in his office behind the store. His widow ran the business for over a year (and made a profit) until the system was in place and she could sell the store. If you have a husband with a business of his own, make it your business to understand it.

Why, why, do men keep their businesses such a deep dark secret from their wives? Four times out of five, the husband dies first and leaves his widow not only bereaved and emotionally bereft but also harried and distraught because she knows nothing of the financial arrangements he has (usually) left in a muddle behind him.

Other Equipment

We call them fiddlies, all these tedious details that you have to attend to, but which once attended to, smooth life's path. So, get yourself a filing cabinet (or box, or expanding file) and a desk and start putting your life in order. What we enjoy is equipping ourselves for action. We love stationery or office supply stores and we happily buy all the little items that make handling the fiddlies easier: paper clips, staples, Scotch tape, labels, lots of pens and pencils, lots of paper and envelopes and file folders, oh, and stamps — lots of stamps — little extra (pretty) folders for current correspondence and bills, cheque book, address book, a calculator and nice rattan baskets for in/out files. These can make the business of running your life much more pleasant and efficient.

Now, if we have managed to brace you for the fiddly part — that is, sorting out your records — we'll get down to details.

Putting Your Financial House In Order

Canadians have the reputation of being people with "shoe-box" mentalities. They like to squirrel things away in shoe-boxes which they then dump out at income-tax time. Some even lug the shoeboxes down to the accountant and pay him/her accounting fees of up to $100 an hour just to sort out the mess. One young man recently wrote about an aunt of his who was $28 out on her bank balance and paid an accountant $200 to find out where the mistake was. It turned out that she had just forgotten to note a $28 withdrawal. What an expensive way to discover that your memory isn't what you hoped it was and what a total misuse of an accountant's time.

To keep that from happening to you, set aside some space somewhere for your financial/household records. If there is no drawer space available, buy two expanding accordion folders and set up your own personal filing system.

Use one file for the current year; the other for things every family should keep on tap.

Current File

There should be sections for:

- household expense receipts (this can cover maintenance and repairs as well as supplies and equipment — anything and everything to do with your home),
- grocery receipts (it's best to separate the food from whatever else you buy at the supermarket so that you can get an accurate picture of what you pay for food, for cleaning supplies, for paper products, for magazines, for cigarettes and for liquor. As with the household expense receipt section, you can lump everything in together and sort it out once every few months or actually subtitle some sections to cover the different types of receipts),
- medical/dental/prescription receipts,
- personal care receipts (you can include notes here on weekly or monthly allowances as well as bills for haircuts, perms, shampoo, cosmetics, etc.),
- clothing receipts (dry cleaning as well as purchases),
- child-care receipts (from both permanent and part-time baby-sitters, nursery school or private kindergartens),
- entertainment receipts (subscriptions, cultural event tickets),
- car expense receipts (gas, repairs, insurance),
- credit card receipts (to check against the monthly bill),
- unpaid current bills,
- paid current bills (hydro, gas, water, etc.),

151

- salary statements (usually the other part of your cheque which shows all your current deductions),
- RRSP and RHOSP receipts,
- current bank statements/cancelled cheques/cheque books/bank books,
- copy of your current budget with monthly updates,
- current net-worth statement.

This is just a suggested list. You can add sections for anything else you need to keep track of on a current basis.

Buy the folder, label it and use it! Keep it handy so everyone in the family knows where it is and what it is for. As the mail comes in or you walk in the door from a shopping expedition, drop all your pertinent bills, receipts, and so on right into their own sections.

Permanent Files

The second folder should be used to store:

- last year's income-tax returns (handy when you go to do this year's),
- past net-worth statements,
- a sheet showing the names, addresses and phone numbers of your doctor(s), dentist, accountant, lawyer, investment dealer, insurance agent, and so on,
- a list of current bank accounts: numbers and banks,
- a list of RHOSP and RRSP accounts: numbers and addresses,
- original marriage licence and birth certificates,
- divorce decree and adoption papers (if applicable),
- a note of the number and the site of your safety deposit box or boxes with information as to the whereabouts of the key(s) and inventory,
- mortgage discharge (It's amazing how many Canadians have paid off their mortgages but haven't bothered, or don't know how, to get the official paper that says that the house is all theirs. Apply at your local law courts building in person and ask for a discharge. If you let your bank, credit union or trust company do it for you, it can cost more than if you apply yourself.),
- a copy of your current mortgage with notations as to when and where payments are to be made,
- last year's property-tax statement,
- deeds to any rental or holiday property you own,

- details on any and all loans for car, boat, personal purchases,
- a photocopy of your current credit cards,
- a copy and details of your life-insurance policies with the company name, agent's name and address, beneficiaries, policy number,
- a copy of your will or a note about where it can be found,
- details and maturity dates and amounts of term deposits/Guaranteed Investment Certificates presently held,
- list of Canada Savings Bonds with maturity dates,
- details on any and all tax shelters (MURBS, gas and oil drilling funds, films, research and development shelters, etc.),
- letter of instruction in case of your death,
- any booklets or leaflets you have picked up or clippings from newspapers on tax information that you think might be useful when it comes to doing your income tax (like Topsy, this can be a section that "just growed," so go through the accumulation often and discard what is out-of-date or not applicable),
- household inventory/appraisals with a copy of your household-content insurance,
- car-insurance policy,
- anything else you want to keep within easy reach.

Everyone's file folders will be individually developed. No one can tell you exactly what it is best for you to keep and in the beginning you will probably keep everything. Over time you will learn what you need to have and can cut back or add accordingly.

Income-Tax Time

Income-tax time comes along with monotonous regularity every spring. When the buds are beginning to burst and we know winter is almost over for another year, it is time to wrestle with tax forms. The system is so complicated that the federal government sends out a 54-page booklet with the forms, explaining all the ins and outs of completing them.

The booklet is explicit. It tells you exactly what to have on hand, warns about problems if you photocopy receipts rather than send originals and explains what to do when information slips are missing. It even admonishes you to detach and complete the working copy first. Arm yourself with sharpened pencil, large eraser, the working copy and the booklet and start going through the forms, sheet by sheet, item by item. The booklet explains each section to you as you go along.

Doing your own income tax is not easy, but once it is finished you feel a real glow of accomplishment. You are finally on top of your financial affairs — at least for last year.

If you aren't at all sure of your arithmetic, try to do it yourself but have the final version checked out by a tax expert or accountant before you send it off in the mail. Mistakes can cost you money and hold up your refund, sometimes for months.

It is only by doing your own tax forms that you will realize how much of your money goes where: to medical bills, charities, union or professional fees, income taxes and so on. It is often a much-needed eye-opener for people who have never thought about where their money goes.

If you need help to complete your form or have specific questions to ask, visit your nearest taxation office. Staffers aren't allowed to fill in the blanks but they can give you advice and information. Remember to get the name and title (if there is one) of the person you speak to. Then if that section of your form is questioned, you at least have someone you can go back to for further information.

Income-Tax Tips

1. Check on what has to be declared as income. Lottery winnings, child tax credits, guaranteed income supplements, a spousal allowance, veteran's disability and dependent pensioners' payments, a war vet's allowance, welfare payments and workers' compensation benefits are not taxable.

2. Include as income everything you get from your employment as well as taxable allowances and benefits, commissions and tips, adult training allowances, net research grants, income maintenance, insurance-plan monies, dividends, family-allowance payments, annuity income, bond, bank and mortgage interest on any investment mortgage you may hold.

3. Remember to declare all the bank interest you received during the year. Banks usually send you T-5s if you earned $50 or more but you are legally responsible to declare everything under $50 as well — the $3.15 you got in interest from one account, the $42.99 from another. Apparently it's all on a computer somewhere and the government knows which button to push; so play it straight and don't add to the delay in getting the tax process over for yet another year.

4. If you have compound interest Canada Savings Bonds (the interest is added every year but not paid to you until the bond actually matures), declare the compound interest on an annual

basis. That means include it even if you didn't get it. Then when the bond matures, most of the interest you get will not be taxable. For example, if you have $1,000 worth of CSBs maturing in 1985, you will get back your original investment of $1,000 and perhaps up to $1,200 in interest. If you have declared your interest all along, there will only be the final year's interest to add to your income for that year; if you have not been declaring the interest every year, the whole $1,200 will become 1985 income. That could put you into a higher tax bracket and add considerably to your tax burden. However, by declaring it annually, the amount you declare every year can be part of that investment-income deduction whereby the first $1,000 you earn in interest, dividends or capital gains is tax-free.

5. Take advantage of all the tax deductions the government allows — RHOSP, RRSP, investment-income deduction, medical deduction, child-care deduction, and so on. It is amazing how many people "forget" or just don't understand some of the deductions. Go over the rules and regulations very carefully and make sure that, if you don't understand what you are entitled to, you ask someone more knowledgeable, or the tax department, to explain matters to you.

6. Up to April 1983, all tax-payers were able to take a standard $100 medical/charitable-donation deduction. The finance minister, Marc Lalonde, eliminated that deduction in his spring 1983 budget but noted that Canadians could still deduct actual charitable donations and medical costs by including receipts with their income tax forms. At the time of writing this legislation had not yet been passed by the House of Commons.

7. Did you know your safety-deposit-box rental is deductible? If you keep your stocks and bonds in it, it's to protect your income property.

$40,090 Income, Tax-Free

Under present tax laws, a single tax-payer in 1983 will be able to earn up to $40,090 and not pay one cent of tax. The catch is that the income must all be in dividends. It would take about $400,000 invested in dividend-bearing stocks to return that amount of money. However, it's a goal to aim at, particularly when you know that the same amount earned in interest or salary would, in 1983, result in a tax bill ranging from a low of about $10,500 in Alberta to a high of more than $14,230

155

in Quebec. The average in the other provinces and territories is about $11,500.

Here's how it works:

Income: (all dividends)	$40,090	
gross-up (when you report dividend income you must report 50 per cent more than what you actually receive)	20,045	
Total income:		$60,135
Deductions: Basic personal	3,770	
Charitable/medical	100*	
Income investment	1,000	
Total Deductions:		4,870
TAXABLE INCOME		$55,265
Federal tax on $55,265	$13,631	
Dividend tax credit	13,631	
Federal tax payable	–0–	
Provincial tax payable	–0–	

Calculations

Dividend tax credit: 34 per cent of original dividend ($40,090) = .34 × $40,090 = $13,631.

Federal tax: tax on $33,012 to $56,592, taxable income, is $6,956 on the first $33,012 plus 30 per cent of the rest. That would mean there would be a tax of $6,956 + 30% ($55,265 − $33,012) =
$6,956 + $6,675 =
$13,631.

---

*Although the $100 charitable/medical deduction was eliminated in the 1983 budget, we have assumed that someone in this income bracket would have contributed at least $100 to charity or have $100 in medical bills to write off.

This example does not include any surtaxes, other credits or the basic federal tax reduction.

Using a dividend tax credit this way is a great help in allowing the rich to get richer. Father, mother and endless numbers of relatives may all report the $40,090 in income without attracting any tax, as long as all the income is in dividends.

People keep asking why nobody tells them about all this. Think about it — most people go to friends or to their bank managers for financial advice. The friends probably don't know much more than you do and your bank manager has a vested interest in keeping your money in his bank.

Again, as always, it's up to you to find out about these things, weigh alternatives and make up your own mind what is best for you. If you do decide to try the dividend route, remember to stick to the tried and true — the Bell Canadas, utilities, banks and so on. Not only do these stocks have an excellent track record in most cases as far as safety of capital is concerned, they also have often issued retractable-preferred shares, which feature returns of 10 per cent to 12 per cent.

Income Splitting

In too many Canadian families it is common to have all of the family investments held by the husbands. Often he "owns" everything because:

- he earned the money and is therefore entitled to have it invested in his name;
- he is the head of the family.

Bad reasoning.

In a two-income family, both husband and wife contribute to living costs and savings accounts; in a family where the wife is a homemaker, she pays her way by making it possible for her spouse to work, knowing his home and children are being cared for properly.

In some families these arguments don't make a dent, but many husbands may respond to the fact that under present tax laws it makes economic sense (and cuts the family taxes) if wives invest in their own names. Also, as people retire with better pensions they face higher income taxes. Therefore, it's more sensible for a husband to receive and pay taxes on pension income, his wife to have the family investment income and pay taxes on that.

If, for example, the family gets $10,000 in pension income and $10,000 in investment income in the husband's name, he would have to pay taxes on the whole $20,000 minus deductions. If, on the other hand, he pays taxes only on his pension and his wife holds the investments and pays the taxes on that $10,000, the total tax bill drops dramatically. The process is known as "income splitting."

How To Do It

Income splitting takes time, effort, money and documentation, but the results are more than worth it. Done properly it can cut taxes and add to a family's income year after year.

Giving money to a spouse or a minor child to invest doesn't achieve the same thing as lending it. Such gifts mean that, although an investment is in another name, the person who did the giving is still responsible for paying the taxes on the money earned by the investment. Nothing is gained.

With a loan it is different. A husband can lend money to his wife to invest. The income is then her tax problem. Up to now there has been no limit on either the amount of the loan allowed or the number of times a loan can be made.

To achieve true income splitting, the wife has to sign a promissory note that can be used, if need be, to convince Revenue Canada that the loan is legitimate and that the borrower fully intends to repay the loan at some time in the future.

The note is as simple as this:

> I, _____, the undersigned, do hereby promise to repay, on demand, and without interest, the sum of $_____ to _____.
> Signature _____ Witness _____
> Date _____

A note like this is good for six years. You can add 15 years to its lifespan (a total of 21 years in all) if you put a legal seal on it (you can buy seals at your local drug store) or draw a small circle and put the letters ''l s'' inside.

Note that it says ''interest free'' and that you will ''pay on demand.'' You can, if you wish, write in a repayment schedule that calls for you to repay five per cent of the loan each year, or a specific amount on the anniversary date.

Keep copies of the note, the cheque and the order for whatever investment is being made. Just to make double sure Revenue Canada won't be upset, make sure your husband writes his cheque on his own account rather than on your joint one and that you put the money into an account under your own name.

If a repayment scheme is part of the agreement, make sure each payment is duly recorded and signed for.

You have to prove to the income tax department that you *intend* to repay — even if it takes forever. Your repayments to your husband are not part of his income. He has already paid tax on the money he lent you. Even the feds can't tax the same money twice, though they might like to.

Repayment does not have to be part of the original agreement. You must be able to prove that the exchange of money is a loan only and that you fully intend to repay your husband ''in the future.'' Whenever it is.

158

The advantages of income splitting are numerous:

- the wife gets some money to invest in her own name and has an income as long as she holds the investments
- the family income tax should go down with both spouses taking advantage of various deductions
- there will be more money in the family pot each year because of the reduced taxes and increased income
- the wife will learn how to handle money and invest it and if widowed will be in a better position to take charge of her own affairs.

A disadvantage is that the husband may lose the spousal deduction for his wife once her investments start to bring her a sizable income of her own. However, the advantages usually far outweigh this disadvantage.

Another form of income splitting is the use of a spousal Registered Retirement Savings Plan. This ploy can be used to spread the income more evenly throughout the family, particularly during retirement years.

Income Splitting with a Minor Child

It is more complicated to split income with a minor child and usually involves a trust, which must be set up by a lawyer. In this instance it is far better to be safe than sorry: get legal advice before you start. Don't let the complications deter you if you think that such income splitting will be to your advantage. Just find out what has to be done and get the best possible person to do it for you.

Another Twist

A relatively new form of income splitting is to have a parent, grandparent, godparent, or other benefactor put up to $5,500 a year in an RRSP in a child's name.

The contribution won't be tax deductible but the interest or other income generated by the money compounds untaxed and the child can cash the plan in at college time when he/she needs the money. Naturally, the proceeds, including the original capital, will be taxed but the child probably won't have any other income at the time and the tax rate should be quite low.

There is a penalty of one per cent per month for the amount paid into an RRSP in excess of allowable contributions, but so far the penalty applies to plans set up for a tax-payer or his or her spouse. According to the experts, a plan for a child is not outlawed at the moment and contributions to it should not be penalized.

159

However, if the idea appeals to you, check it out with your accountant to make sure you do it properly. Revenue Canada has been known to come down hard on people who, in its view, are abusing regulations.

Helpful Hints to Simplify Tax Preparation

1. Use your cheque-book as your record book for everything. Put all your money into your chequing account first, even though you transfer most of it immediately to daily-interest or premium savings. Pay all your bills by cheque, and make a note in your cheque-book as to the reason/purpose of the expenditure. Never use anything but your own personal cheque (it's almost impossible not to these days — something to do with magnetized ink). When you transfer funds to other accounts, do so by cheque.

2. Keep all your receipts for items that you know you can claim as deductible expenses. We know some people who simply dump them all into a big brown manila envelope for the year and then sit down with a drink and sort them out on Doomsday. Others, more organized, have a file with separate categories: postage, parking, transportation, entertaining. Make sure you know all your deductible expenses.

One More Thing

Even though you've been told it's good for your soul, your morale and your confidence to do your own income-tax return, there are exceptions to every rule and one of us is it. I would rather die than do my own return and I probably would also be sent to jail. "Know thyself" is an old Greek saw and it's still true, true, true. If you can do your own tax return, I'm proud (awestruck, too) of you, but count me out. Besides, the fee I pay my tax accountant is deductible, and the amount of money he saves me by doing it right and knowing what I can claim is worth his fee. He is a magic man and I love him dearly.

A Furry Tale

We know four women, all different shapes, sizes, and ages, who together bought a mink coat for $400 in a second-hand shop, just so they could feel what it was like to wear one, once in a lifetime. They spent $100 for a new lining. After they had each worn it once, they sold the coat for $2,800.

A nice touch here is that if one woman had done this, the government

160

would have demanded part of the profit as capital gains. The federal government is interested in personal property that costs or sells for more than $1,000. In this instance they would have deemed the coat to have cost $1,000 and the profit to be $2,800 − $1,000 = $1,800 with one-half of that, $900 taxable as capital gains at the seller's personal tax rate.

With four people taking part in the transaction, both the buying and the selling price were less than the $1,000 limit and capital gains at that level aren't taxable.

If that isn't a happy ending, what is?

16

As Beautiful as Roses

*"Money, which represents the prose of life,
and which is hardly spoken of in parlors
without an apology, is, in its effects and
laws, as beautiful as roses."*
RALPH WALDO EMERSON

Life at the Bottom Line

You can do it. You've proved you can do anything you want to do, once you set your mind to it. You're finally beginning to feel a surge of confidence and strength as you become more competent in dealing with your financial affairs. And yet, and yet — you still run out of money. Not as often, maybe, but it still gets a little tight from time to time. And you've been scrimping and saving and studying so hard, you begin to wonder where the fun is. You may not have known what you were doing before, but you sure were having a better time.

Hang on. Life at the bottom line doesn't seem to allow much space for personal growth. Even when we get enough, or a little, money, the way our economy is structured, we don't always make the best use of it. The minute you think you're pulling ahead a little, along comes an unexpected bill, emergency or must-have that blows a hole in your carefully planned budget. It's not just you; it happens to everyone. Nineteenth-century writer Samuel Butler commented that "all progress is based on a universal innate desire on the part of every organism to live beyond its income." Welcome to the club.

Troubled Times

It's getting harder for many Canadians to make ends meet. An increasing percentage of families now have one rather than two working parents (the single-parent family, headed by a female, is the fastest-growing family unit today). Young men and women can't find jobs. People who got into financial trouble when interest rates were high as an elephant's eye have never been able to catch up.

Those who have had wages garnisheed know they're in trouble, but what about the rest of us, the ones who have trouble making ends meet because the ends are so much farther apart than they used to be? Watch for these warning signs:

- you can't make it from paycheque to paycheque without borrowing;
- interest charges are piling up because you can't pay off credit cards;
- creditors are threatening legal action or are repossessing;
- you catch yourself thinking that if you just ignore all those bills they will go away.

In other words, you owe your soul to the company store. Insupportable debt is money's way of telling you to stop spending the stuff.

Tackling the Problem

Once you know you're in trouble, discuss the situation with your family and take some positive action as soon as you can:

- list your debts in order of priority, housing first;
- call creditors individually, asking for a meeting;
- show each creditor your monthly income and outgo, and explain that you want to pay off your bills but that you need some help;
- suggest spreading debt payments over a longer period of time, promising to pay a little each month, and the balance when you can;
- if the creditor agrees (and to him/her some money should be better than no money), get the agreement in writing;
- live up to your promises.

Debt Consolidation

Rather than meeting with creditors, some people consolidate their debts by taking out one loan to cover the lot. This usually means a higher rate of interest paid over a longer period of time and actually increases the debt load.

If you want to try this solution, negotiate a loan that can be paid back without penalty at any time. Make a practice of adding a bit to the principal payments as often as you can. Even a couple of extra dollars a month can help to clear the debt more quickly.

Government Help

If things are totally out of hand or if you feel that you can't face creditors, call a provincial government debtors' assistance office and make an appointment. A trained counsellor will meet with you to help sort out the mess and get you on the road to financial recovery.

At your first meeting you will probably have to present recent wage slips, a list of your current assets, expenses and debts and the names and addresses of your creditors.

The counsellor's job is to try to:

- work out a practical budget for you;
- meet with your creditors to discuss an adjustment of payments;
- mediate any disputes you have with your creditors;
- advise whether you should go into bankruptcy and if so, how you should go about it;
- help you to understand how you got into the mess in the first place and suggest ways to ensure it won't happen again.

In short, the counsellor will help you to help yourself.

Keeping your Perspective

All the money-grubbing and consolidating and all the stock-market smarts in the world aren't going to mean much if you don't feel good about yourself. Keep a sense of perspective and a sense of humour about what you're doing. Sniff the flowers, as they say, on the way by. No one said you had to buy hot-house flowers to sniff.

The best things in life aren't free, not these days. Yet there are still gratuitous pleasures, unbought, unbuyable — or for a very cheap price — that will help you along, make every-day life a little more worth living, turn an ordinary day into something special. We don't want to get maudlin about this, so we won't talk about babies' smiles or kittens or fireplaces. We'd like to mention a few sensuous, self-indulgent, personal gifts you can give yourself, habits or things that will help you get through the times when you're feeling terribly deprived.

Keep a list, if you like lists (we love lists!), and haul it out to see what you can do for yourself when you're feeling really bruised by the economy. Our list is personal, of course, and you can add your own special ideas. It starts with the words from the musical, *You're A Good Man, Charlie Brown*. "Happiness is . . . " and you add your own definitions.

Happiness Is . . .

1. The first lilac in the spring. (What did we tell you about sniffing the flowers?) Go ahead and sniff and O.D. on lilac.
2. Taking tea back to bed in the morning. It's worth getting up a little early to have that feeling of pampered luxury.
3. A perfectly poached egg, symmetrically round and white, with a runny yolk, and it has to be eaten immediately, while it's hot.
4. "Free" laundry. If you use coin-operated washing and drying machines, it's a good practice to put your quarters and/or dimes into a box or piggy bank at the end of each day. That way, you always have the right change and it feels quite painless.
5. Pennies similarly saved can go into rolls for the bank. It may be tedious but "Penny wise, pound foolish" is an accurate axiom. Money in a wallet gets spent. Remove it, and temptation, too.
6. Paper, any kind of blank paper, especially free paper. Sometimes you go to a meeting and everyone is given a pad of paper for note-taking. That's nice.
7. Printed paper isn't bad, either. A free newspaper on an airplane, a used one on a subway train or bus, old, odd magazines you seldom see but get to read in doctors' or dentists' waiting rooms — all are fun as are the glamorous foreign ones in the hair salon. Free recipe pamphlets at the supermarket, even advertising brochures in those racks in the shopping malls provide free information.
8. Coupons. Use them, but don't buy products you don't want for the sake of pennies off.
9. Free samples. But you have to be strong-minded and refuse to allow yourself to be pushed into buying something you don't want, can't use.
10. Champagne is wonderful, and good for the morale. You can buy little three-packs (three for about $7.50) in a couple of different brands. Use them by the one — for a happy-birthday toast, or happy divorce, or it's Sunday-with-orange-juice (and a little goes a longer way), without destroying your budget.
11. An apple and a piece of cheese. An apple so crisp you know you've got teeth, and Cheddar so sharp you know you've got some taste buds — the best thing to hit a brown bag for lunch.

12. Waking up too early, checking the time and knowing you have lots more time to sleep.
13. Lighting candles for the first time. But keep on lighting them. Put used candles in your bedroom and light them for special occasions.
14. Horoscopes — a free look into your future.
15. Naps. Anywhere, any time.
16. Re-reading *Gone With the Wind*. Or watching the movie on the late, late show.
17. Screaming in a thirty-miles-per-hour zone. (There's a song about this.) It's more fun on a freeway. Screaming — or singing — at 100 kilometres an hour is very sensuous. It also keeps you awake if you're getting road-drowsy.
18. Getting real letters in the mail. Not notes or cards or bills or ads, but real letters. You can tell how you really feel about someone by your reaction to his/her letter. We feel good about anyone who writes to us.
19. Walking. Cheaper than taking the car, cheaper than the public transit, and it's better for you.
20. Sunshine. (Almost always makes us high.)
21. Picking privileges, as in fruit-picking. Make it a family or group event. You'll save a lot of money and end up with a freezer or a fruit cellar full of summer to last you all winter.
22. Cleaning off your desk.
23. New file folders. In fact —
24. Getting organized (see chapter nine).
25. Saying, "I did it myself."

Doing It Yourself

Doing it yourself, in fact, is back in style and saves money in more ways than meet the eye.

Few of us realize that if we spend $100 having curtains mended we actually have to make more than that to have the $100 to spend.

If you were in a 50-per-cent tax bracket (and very few women in Canada are anywhere close to that), you would actually have to bring in $200 and pay one-half of it, or $100, in taxes to have $100 for the mending.

Closer to home, if you are in the 25-per-cent bracket you would have to make $133.32 with $33.33 going to taxes and the $100 on hand for the drapes.

If you look at all your expenditures from the point of view of how much money you have to earn to have something done, it will be a great incentive to roll up your sleeves, master your sewing machine and dig your own garden. And, if worse comes to worst and you can't cope on your own, trade your special talents with a neighbour who can do what you want done.

Barter

Barter is an increasingly frequent method of exchange. You don't have money, but you have a skill or you have time, and you trade that for a thing or a service that you need. Women with young children do this on a small scale all the time. They trade baby-sitting time with a friend or neighbour who is equally young, poor and surrounded by children. Such a trade is often more rewarding than a mere money exchange because of the human factor involved. It speaks of community spirit and caring for each other.

Barter is not always done on a one-to-one basis. Communities, families or friends can take bartering one step further and set up formal or informal skill exchanges. That means that if you bake the best chocolate cake in town, you may be able to exchange two cakes for hemming drapes. A knitter could swap an Icelandic sweater that would sell for over $100 in return for some plumbing work. A bookkeeper could do your income tax while you planted his/her garden. The variations are endless, and bartering saves a lot of money.

There are sophisticated organizations springing up that keep track of the exchanges and allow units of exchange. Say you're a hairdresser and you do someone's hair. That someone might be a calligrapher, but you don't need the services of a calligrapher right now, thank you. You get credit for the service you've performed. The calligrapher writes a presentation scroll for an appliance-store manager who is retiring one of the employees. You need your toaster repaired. You take it to the appliance store and exchange your credits for that service. Like that. Pretty soon it's going to be big business. Someone has to manage the books, to keep track of the exchanges. And soon the government is going to figure out a way to tax it.

The Cost

"Pride," said Thomas Jefferson, "costs more than hunger, thirst and cold." There's a new kind of pride that weighs even more than material comforts, and though it's harder won, it doesn't cost as much. We're talking about the pride you take in yourself, and justifiably so.

You have proved you can set your own standards and live by them.

168

Simplify your life and profit by it, learn to say enough is enough, to say no, to say "I can't" — and also to say "I can." Women can give up the habit any time of being underpaid, undervalued, second-class citizens. You've been working for your money, one way and another, for a long time now, not forgetting the unpaid housewife. As the Canadian Royal Commission on the Status of Women reported in 1970, "The housewife who remains at home is just as much a producer of goods and services as the paid worker, and in our view she should also have the opportunity to provide for a more financially secure future."

Now you know how to make your money work for you. Use it well. James Robertson, an English management consultant, says that we have to "rethink the meaning of such things as wealth and work," and that we should "move in the direction of personal and social goals rather than keep on building up an accumulation of material success." That, too, but we have to learn how to accumulate and control our money first.

We hope you have fun doing it.

Appendix — Division of Assets

Newfoundland

Legislation

Matrimonial Property Act of 1980 — deferred sharing with judicial discretion (applies to those who have not opted out by marriage contract).

During the Marriage

GENERAL RULE

- Spouses are separate as to property; a wife has no rights over the property or money acquired and owned by her husband.
- If a man buys property for, or transfers property to, his wife, he is still deemed to be the owner unless there is clear proof that he meant it to be a gift.

EXCEPTION(S)

1. The matrimonial home is owned by both spouses jointly, even if only one bought it, inherited it or otherwise acquired it.
2. If property or money is put in the joint names of both spouses, it is considered to be proof that they own it in equal shares.

On Separation or Divorce

ALIMONY/MAINTENANCE

Awarded by the court.

FAMILY ASSETS

- Equal share — the court can vary sharing if it believes equal sharing is "grossly unjust or unconscionable."

- The court may grant ownership of the family home to one spouse, exclusive use to the other, in unusual circumstances.

OTHER ASSETS

Businesses, farm operations, savings, RRSPs are not generally shared unless the non-owning spouse has added to their value through contribution of work or money. In such cases the court will order compensation or share for the non-owning spouse.

On Husband's Death

- A widow has the same right to share assets as on separation or divorce.
- A widow automatically inherits her husband's share of the family home.
- If a widow is inadequately provided for, she may apply to the courts for a larger share of her husband's estate.

Prince Edward Island

Legislation

Family Law Reform Act of 1979 — deferred sharing with judicial discretion (applies to those who don't opt out by marriage contract, except for the provisions covering the matrimonial home, which apply to everyone during marriage).

During the Marriage

GENERAL RULE

- Spouses are separate as to property; a wife has no rights over the property or money acquired and owned by her husband.
- If a man buys property for, or transfers property to, his wife, he is still deemed to be the owner unless there is clear proof that he meant it to be a gift.

EXCEPTION(S)

1. The matrimonial home can't be sold or mortgaged without the consent of both spouses or a court order.
2. Both spouses are equally entitled to use the family home, even if it is owned by only one.
3. If property or money is put in the joint names of both spouses, it is considered to be proof that they own it in equal shares.

On Separation or Divorce

ALIMONY/MAINTENANCE

Awarded by the court.

FAMILY ASSETS
- Equal share.
- The court can vary the sharing if it feels equal sharing would be inequitable.
- The court may grant ownership of the family home to one spouse and exclusive use to the other. This is done only in exceptional circumstances.

OTHER ASSETS
- Businesses, farms, savings, pension rights and RRSPs are not generally shared unless:
    1. a spouse liquidated family assets to avoid sharing;
    2. the spouse who does not own non-family assets has contributed work or money to increase their value;
    3. the court decides it would be inequitable not to share.

On Husband's Death
- Sharing of property occurring on separation or divorce does not apply for a widow unless the couple was already separated or divorced and an action for splitting had been started before death.
- If a widow is left inadequately provided for, she can apply to the court for a larger share of her husband's estate.

Nova Scotia

Legislation
Matrimonial Property Act of 1980 — deferred sharing with judicial discretion (applies to those who do not opt out by marriage contract).

During the Marriage
GENERAL RULE
- Spouses are separate as to property; a wife has no rights over property or money acquired and owned by her husband.
- If a man buys property in his wife's name or transfers it to her, he is still deemed to be the owner unless there is clear proof that it was meant to be a gift.

EXCEPTION(S)
1. The matrimonial home cannot be sold or mortgaged without the consent of both spouses or a court order.
2. Both spouses are equally entitled to use the family home even if it is owned by only one.
3. If property or money is held in the joint names of both spouses, it is considered proof they own it in equal shares.

On Separation or Divorce
ALIMONY/MAINTENANCE
>   Awarded by the court.

FAMILY ASSETS
* Equal share.
* The court can vary the sharing to avoid an "unfair and unconscionable" result.
* The court may grant ownership of the family home to one spouse, exclusive use to the other. This to be done only in exceptional circumstances.

OTHER ASSETS
* The spouse receives a share of any assets or other compensation, if she has contributed work or money to increase the value of her husband's business assets.

On Husband's Death
* The widow has the same right to a share of assets as on separation or divorce.
* If a widow is not adequately provided for, she may apply to the court for a larger share of her husband's estate.

New Brunswick

Legislation
>   The Marital Property Act of 1981 — deferred sharing with judicial discretion (applies to those who do not opt out by marriage contract).

During the Marriage
GENERAL RULE
* Spouses are separate as to property; a wife has no rights over the property or money acquired and owned by her husband.
* If a man buys property in his wife's name or transfers it to her, he is still said to be the owner unless there is clear proof that he meant it to be a gift.

EXCEPTION(S)
1. The matrimonial home can't be sold without the consent of both spouses or a court order.
2. Both spouses are equally entitled to use the home and its contents, even if only one owns it.
3. When the home is sold, each spouse is entitled to half the net proceeds although, if equal shares are considered to be "inequitable," either spouse can ask for another division from the court.

4. If property or money is put in joint names of both spouses, it is considered to be proof that they own it in equal shares.

On Separation or Divorce

ALIMONY/MAINTENANCE

Awarded by the court.

FAMILY ASSETS

- Equal share — the court can vary the sharing to avoid what it considers "inequities."
- The court may grant ownership of the family home to one spouse and give exclusive use to the other, but this is only done in exceptional circumstances.

OTHER ASSETS

- Equal share of everything acquired during marriage, except for businesses, gifts or inheritances.
- The court can vary the sharing to avoid what it considers to be "inequities."
- For property not generally shareable — businesses, gifts, inheritances — the court may decide to grant a share to a non-owning spouse:
  1. if one spouse sold marital property to avoid sharing;
  2. if the court believes it would be inequitable not to share, especially if the assumption by one spouse of child-care and household work affected the other's ability to acquire, manage, maintain, operate or improve property;
  3. if a spouse has contributed work or money to increase the value of the other's business.

On Husband's Death

- A widow has the same rights as on separation or divorce.
- If a widow is not left adequately provided for, she can apply to the courts for a larger share of her husband's estate.

Quebec

Legislation

The standard matrimonial regime in Quebec is called "partnership of assets" — deferred sharing (applies to those who married after July 1970, who do not opt out through a marriage contract).

During the Marriage

GENERAL RULE

- Spouses are separate as to property; a wife has no rights over the property or money acquired and owned by her husband.

EXCEPTION(S)
1. A spouse can't give away property or money earned during the marriage, except for small amounts or presents, without the other spouse's consent.
2. A spouse can't move out of, sell or dispose of the contents of the matrimonial home used for family purposes, without the other spouse's consent.
3. A matrimonial home against which one spouse has filed a "declaration of family residence" can't be rented, sold or mortgaged without the consent of both spouses or a court order.

On Separation or Divorce
ALIMONY/MAINTENANCE
Awarded by the court.
FAMILY ASSETS AND OTHER ASSETS
- Absolute right to one-half of all assets acquired by her husband during the time of their marriage. This usually means equal division of all assets. The only exceptions are gifts, inheritances, awards for damages, rights to future pensions and personal items.
- The court can grant exclusive use of family furniture to either spouse, sometimes with financial consideration to the other.

On Husband's Death
- A widow has the same right to a share of assets as on separation or divorce.
- A widow has no legal recourse to a larger share of the estate until a provision enacted in 1981 is proclaimed, enabling her to apply for a compensatory payment for contributions in work or money that increased the value of her husband's property.
- There are several other measures proposed, but not yet enacted, that would affect a widow's position in Quebec.

(Note: other provisions enacted, but not proclaimed, would allow the courts to give the use of the family home to the non-owning spouse; and at the time of divorce, either spouse could be ordered to make payments to the other to compensate for his/her contribution in money or work to the increase in the value of the other's property. When this last provision is proclaimed, the standard matrimonial regime in Quebec will change from simple deferred sharing to deferred sharing with judicial discretion.)

176

Ontario

Legislation

Family Law Reform Acts of 1975, 1978 — deferred sharing with judicial discretion (applies to spouses who do not opt out of it by marriage contract except for the matrimonial home provisions which, during marriage, apply to everyone).

During the Marriage

GENERAL RULE

- Spouses are separate as to property; a wife has no rights over the property or money acquired and owned by her husband.
- If a man buys property in his wife's name or transfers it to her, he is deemed to be the owner unless there is clear proof that it was meant to be a gift.

EXCEPTION(S)

1. Matrimonial home cannot be sold or mortgaged without the consent of both spouses or a court order.
2. Both spouses are equally entitled to use the matrimonial home, even if one is listed as owner of that home.
3. If property or money is put in joint names of the spouses, it is considered to be proof that they own it in equal shares.

On Separation or Divorce

ALIMONY/MAINTENANCE

Awarded by the court.

FAMILY ASSETS

- Equal share.
- The court has the discretion to vary the sharing if it believes equal sharing would be "inequitable."
- The court can grant ownership of the family home to one spouse, exclusive use to the other (in exceptional circumstances only).

OTHER ASSETS

- Businesses, farm operations, RRSPs and pension rights are not generally shared unless:
  1. one spouse sold family assets to avoid sharing;
  2. the spouse not owning family assets has contributed work or money to increase their value;
  3. one spouse has assumed child-care and housework responsibilities to enhance the other spouse's ability to acquire, maintain or improve non-family assets;
  4. the court decides it would inequitable not to share some of these other assets.

177

On Husband's Death
- Sharing as on separation or divorce does not apply unless the couple is already separated or divorced and an action for splitting property had been begun before death.
- If a widow is not left sufficient to provide adequately for herself, she can apply to the court for a larger share of her husband's estate.

Manitoba

Legislation
Marital Property Act of 1978 — deferred sharing with judicial discretion (applies to those who do not opt out of it by marriage contract).

During the Marriage
GENERAL RULE
- Spouses are separate as to property; a wife has no rights over property or money acquired and owned by her husband.

EXCEPTION(S)
1. Homestead rights ensure that a spouse who owns the family home and the land on which it stands — up to 320 acres in some cases — must have his/her spouse's written consent before selling or mortgaging.
2. A husband who buys property in his wife's name, or transfers it to her, is deemed to have made a gift of it to her, and if he later tries to reclaim it, he has to have proof that it was not meant as a gift.*
3. Spouses are equally entitled to use the family home, contents, car, cottage and other things used for family living, even if only one owns them.
4. Homemaking wives are entitled to, in addition to such usual spousal rights as food, shelter, clothing, a reasonable cash allowance for personal expenses to be paid to them by their wage-earning husbands.
5. Each spouse has the right, enforceable by court order, to detailed information about the other spouse's financial affairs, including wages and debts.

On Separation or Divorce
ALIMONY/MAINTENANCE
Awarded by the court.

FAMILY ASSETS

- Equal share.
- The court has discretion to vary shares if it believes the result would otherwise be "grossly unfair or unconscionable" because of "extraordinary circumstances."
- Family assets in Manitoba include car, home, contents, cottage, other things used for family purposes and rights to both pension plans and private insurance policies.
- The court may award ownership of the home to one spouse, exclusive use to the other.

OTHER ASSETS

- Equal share, except for those acquired before marriage by one spouse for his/her exclusive use.
- Other assets would include farm operations, savings, businesses, and so on, and the court has discretion to vary sharing if it finds equal sharing to be clearly "inequitable."

On Husband's Death

The Dower Act prevails and entitles the surviving spouse to one-half the estate, up to $250,000 or $15,000 per year.

- The surviving spouse also has a "life estate" in the homestead (the home and up to 320 acres of land), giving her the right to live there for the rest of her life or to collect rents from it.
- If a widow is not sufficiently provided for, she can apply to the court for a larger share of her husband's estate.

* Interestingly enough, in Manitoba, British Columbia and the Northwest Territories, the same rule does not apply to transfers from wives to husbands. In those cases, the wife is still considered to be the owner unless and until there is clear proof that she meant it as a gift.

Saskatchewan

Legislation

Matrimonial Property Act of 1980 — deferred sharing with judicial discretion (applies to spouses who do not opt out of it by marriage contract).

During the Marriage

GENERAL RULE

- Spouses are separate as to property, so a wife has no rights over property or money acquired and owned by her husband.
- If a man buys property in his wife's name or transfers it to

179

her, he is still deemed to own it unless there is clear proof that it was meant to be a gift.

EXCEPTION(S)

1. Homestead rights ensure that a husband can't sell or mortgage the matrimonial home he owns or the land on which it stands (up to 160 acres in some cases) without his wife's written consent.
2. Both spouses are equally entitled to use the home and contents, even if they are held in one name.
3. If property or money is held in joint names of the spouses, it is considered proof that they own it in equal shares.
4. During the marriage a spouse can apply to the courts for a division of matrimonial property, with the splitting done on the same basis as in separation or divorce.

On Separation or Divorce

ALIMONY/MAINTENANCE

Awarded by the court.

FAMILY ASSETS

- Equal share — the court has discretion to vary the sharing or to share excluded assets.
- The court may grant ownership of the family home to one spouse, exclusive use to the other.
- The court must maintain the equal shares of the family home unless this would give ''unfair and inequitable'' results because of the need of the spouse who has custody of the children.

OTHER ASSETS

- Equal share.
- The only exceptions are assets acquired before the marriage by one spouse for his/her exclusive use.
- The court has discretion to vary the sharing or to share excluded assets.

On Husband's Death

- The widow has the same rights as under divorce or separation.
- Permission of the widow is still needed to sell or mortgage the matrimonial home and land — up to 160 acres in some cases. This often means she retains possession of the home during her lifetime or renounces the right to prevent disposition in exchange for other considerations.
- If a widow is not sufficiently provided for, she can apply to the court for a larger share of her husband's estate.

Alberta

Legislation

Matrimonial Property Act of 1979 — deferred sharing with judicial discretion (applies to those who have not opted out of it by marriage contract).

During the Marriage

GENERAL RULE

- Spouses are separate as to property; a wife has no rights over property or money acquired and owned by her husband.
- If a man buys property in his wife's name or transfers property to her name, he is still deemed to be the owner of the property unless there is clear proof that he meant it to be a gift.

EXCEPTION(S)

1. Homestead rights prevent the spouse who owns the family home and the land on which it stands (up to 160 acres in some cases) from mortgaging or selling them without the written consent of the other spouse.
2. If property or money is in the joint names of the spouses, it is considered to be proof they own it in equal shares.

ALIMONY/MAINTENANCE

Awarded by the court.

FAMILY ASSETS AND OTHER ASSETS

- Equal share of spouses' property acquired during marriage, except under special circumstances.
- Sharing is subject to the discretion of the court.
- The court may grant ownership of the matrimonial home and contents to one spouse, but exclusive use to the other.

On Husband's Death

- Sharing as for separation or divorce can't take place unless couple was already separated, divorced or divorce action was under way. If so, the survivor can apply to the courts for sharing within six months of validation of the will.
- If the surviving wife is not eligible for sharing, she has a special property right to a "life estate" in the homestead and contents. Even if her husband willed the property to someone else, she can live there or rent it out for the rest of her life.
- If a widow is not sufficiently provided for, she can ask the court for a larger share of her husband's estate.

181

British Columbia

Legislation

Family Relations Act of 1979 — a regime of deferred sharing with judicial discretion (applies to spouses who do not opt out of it by contract).

During the Marriage

GENERAL RULE

- Spouses are separate as to property; a wife has no rights over property or money acquired and owned by her husband.

EXCEPTION(S)

1. If a wife registers her right over the family home and land on which it stands, neither can be mortgaged or sold without her consent or a court order.
2. A husband is presumed to have made a gift of property or money to his wife if he buys it or transfers it to her — if he later wants to claim this property or money as his own, he must prove that he did not mean to give the property or money to her.*

On Separation or Divorce

ALIMONY/MAINTENANCE

Awarded by the court.

FAMILY ASSETS

- Equal share, including car, home, contents, things used for family purposes, pension rights, RHOSP, RRSPs.
- Sharing is subject to the discretion of the courts in cases where it considers the sharing to be unjust or inequitable.

OTHER ASSETS

- Business assets and other investments are not usually shareable unless the spouse who doesn't have them has contributed directly (work or money) or indirectly (family care, household work) to their acquisition.

On Husband's Death

- Sharing of property on separation or divorce does not apply. If a widow is disinherited to the point that she can't support herself adequately, she can ask the court for a larger share of her husband's estate.

Northwest Territories

Legislation

Matrimonial Property Ordinance of 1974 — a regime of judicial discretion (applies to those who did not opt out by special formal agreements).

During the Marriage
GENERAL RULE
- Spouses are separate as to property; a wife has no rights over the property or money acquired and owned by her husband.

EXCEPTION(S)
1. If a husband buys property in his wife's name or transfers it to her, he is said to have made a gift of it to her. If he later wants to reclaim it, he has to prove that it was not meant as a gift.
2. At any time during the marriage either spouse can ask the court for a division of matrimonial property, with splitting done on the same basis as in the case of divorce or separation.*

On Separation or Divorce
ALIMONY/MAINTENANCE
Awarded by the court.

FAMILY ASSETS AND OTHER ASSETS
- The court is fully empowered to redistribute property between the spouses in what it considers to be a "fair and equitable" manner.
- Judges have almost full discretion.

On Husband's Death
- No provision exists to split matrimonial property on the husband's death.
- Provisions enacted, but not proclaimed, from the Ordinance of 1974 would entitle surviving spouses to a "life estate" in the matrimonial home and the land on which it sits — up to 160 acres in some cases — as well as in some of the personal effects of the deceased.

*In the Northwest Territories, the legislation contains provisions preventing a spouse from selling or mortgaging the family home without the consent of the other spouse, but this has not been proclaimed as yet.

Yukon

Legislation
Matrimonial Property Ordinance of 1980 — deferred sharing with judicial discretion (applies to those who do not opt out by marriage

contract, except for provisions regarding the family home, which apply to everyone during marriage).

During the Marriage

GENERAL RULE

- Spouses are separate as to property; a wife has no rights over the property or money acquired and owned by her husband.
- If a man buys property for, or transfers it to, his wife, he is deemed still to be the owner unless here is clear proof that he meant it as a gift.

EXCEPTIONS

1. The matrimonial home can't be sold or mortgaged without the consent of both spouses or a court order.
2. Both spouses are equally entitled to use the home, regardless of which one owns it.
3. If property or money is put in the joint names of both spouses, it is considered to be proof they own it in equal shares.

On Separation or Divorce

ALIMONY/MAINTENANCE

Awarded by the court.

FAMILY ASSETS

- Equal sharing.
- The court may vary sharing if it believes equal sharing would be "inequitable."
- Under exceptional circumstances the court may award ownership of the family home to one spouse, exclusive use to the other.

OTHER ASSETS

- Businesses, farms, savings, pensions are not generally shared unless:
    1. one spouse liquidated family assets to avoid sharing;
    2. the non-owning spouse has contributed work or money to increase the value of the assets;
    3. the "assumption by one spouse of all child-care and housework responsibilities" has enhanced the other spouse's ability to acquire, maintain or improve non-family assets;
    4. the court decides it would be inequitable not to share some of the other assets.

On Husband's Death

- Sharing of property as on separation or divorce does not apply

on death, unless the couple was already separated or divorced and an action for splitting property had already been started.
- If a widow cannot support herself adequately, she can apply to the court for a larger share of her husband's estate.

Glossary of Investment and Insurance Terms

Accidental-death benefit —
paid when death is caused
directly by accidental bodily
injury. Called a "double
indemnity" benefit if it is
attached to a life policy of the
same face amount.

*Accident and sickness
insurance* — various kinds of
insurance offering benefits for
loss of income or expenses
resulting from accidental
injury, sickness or from
accidental death.

Account Executive — securities
salesperson; registered
representative; stock broker.

Actuary — someone
professionally trained in the
mathematical and the
technical aspects of life

insurance, pensions and
related fields, such as the
calculation of premiums,
reserves and other values.

Adjusted cost base — the cost
from which capital gains and
capital losses are calculated
for income-tax purposes.

Agent — sales and service
representative of a life
insurance company, often
called a life underwriter.

Annuitant — usually a person
receiving annuity income, but
in strict terms the person
during whose lifetime the
income is payable.

Annuity — a life annuity is a
contract providing periodic
payments during the life of an
annuitant. Often payments are
guaranteed for a minimum
period, for example, five, 10

*Insurance terms are starred.

187

or 15 years. Annuities can also be bought with survivor benefits, which means that payments will continue until the death of the last person named as an annuitant. An agreement under which assets are turned over to an institution on the condition the donor, or other designated person, receive specified regular payments for a specified period of time.

Annuity certain — a contract providing periodic payments for a specified number of years, not dependent on any person's survival.

Annuity consideration — a payment, or one of the regular periodic payments, made to buy an annuity.

Appreciation — the increase in an item's value over the years.

Arbitrage — a buying and selling technique used to take advantage of price differences for the same stock traded on different markets. For example, buying stock on the Toronto Stock Exchange and selling it at almost the same time for more on the New York Stock Exchange.

Ask — the price at which a stockholder is willing to sell his/her shares.

Assets — any items you own — house, car, furniture, stocks, bonds, and so on — that have value.

Asset value — the monetary value of holdings.

*Assignment — transfer by the owner of a legal right or interest in a life-insurance policy to someone else. May be done for collateral purposes as security for a debt.

*Assurance — term for insurance used mostly by British-based companies.

At the Market — an order to buy or sell securities at the existing market price rather than at a specific price.

*Automatic premium loan — provides that any premium for permanent life insurance not paid at the end of the grace period will be paid automatically by a loan on the policy.

Average or index — for stocks, indicators of broad market performance. The Dow Jones industrial average includes the shares of thirty large U.S. companies; the Toronto Stock Exchange's composite index covers 300 companies.

Averaging down — buying more of a security or commodity at a price lower than the original price to reduce the average cost per unit.

Bear — someone who believes stock prices are going to go down.

*Beneficiary — person entitled to the insurance money when the person insured dies.

Bid — the price a buyer is prepared to pay to purchase shares.

Blue chips — companies, or shares of companies, regarded over a long period of time as financially sound and well managed.

Bond — a certificate of indebtedness issued by a government or company. A bondholder actually loans money to the issuer and is paid interest on the bond he holds.

Bottom line — net profit — the amount left after all bills, taxes, and so on are paid.

Broker — an agent who handles orders to buy or sell securities and by so doing earns a commission.

Bull — someone who believes stock prices are going to go up.

Call — an option for which the buyer pays a premium for the right to purchase 100 shares of a particular stock at a specific price, within a stated period of time of up to nine months.

Capital — money accumulated for investment or retirement purposes.

Capital gain — a profit on the sale of a capital asset.

Cash account — a client's account with a financial institution, to be settled on a strictly cash basis.

*Cash surrender value — cash available when an owner voluntarily cancels a policy.

*Cash value life insurance — life insurance providing cash surrender value when the policy is cancelled.

Cats and dogs — companies, or securities of companies, of doubtful value.

Certificate of Deposit (CD) — a specified amount of money left on deposit with a bank for a stated period of time which earns interest at more than the minimum passbook rate.

Certified cheque — a cheque guaranteed to be good because the bank withdraws the funds from the account when it draws the cheque.

Collectibles — objects that may be collected for pleasure or practical purposes as well as possible appreciation as an investment; for example, art, stamps, antiques, coins, comic books.

Commodities — contracts for the purchase or sale of fixed amounts of wheat, cocoa, orange juice, soya beans, silver, plywood, pork bellies, and so on, traded for immediate delivery (the cash or spot market) or for future delivery (the futures market).

Common stock — a share in the ownership of a corporation, giving you the right to vote at shareholders' meetings and to receive any dividends declared.

*Conditional receipt — given to an insurance applicant who pays a premium with the application. If the insurance is assessed at standard rates, the coverage, up to a certain limit, begins at the time set out in the receipt rather than when the policy is delivered.

Convertible — a feature of some securities that allows the owner to turn the securities into another class according to certain conditions.

*Convertible term insurance — may be exchanged for a permanent life insurance policy without providing evidence of insurability.

*Creditor's group insurance — life insurance issued on the lives of customers of banks and other institutional lenders naming the institution as beneficiary, to pay off any debt if the customer dies.

*Date of issue — when the company issued the policy.

*Death benefit — paid when the person insured dies.

Debenture — a form of bond not secured by a specific asset but reflecting the general financial strength of the company.

*Decreasing term insurance — term insurance in which the face amount decreases over the term of the policy.

*Deductible — the amount you must pay on a claim before your insurance company begins to make payments.

Deed — a document used to transfer ownership of property from one person (the seller) to another (the buyer).

*Deferred annuity — an annuity in which interest income accumulates for a period before payments begin. The period may total several years.

Deposit Certificate, Deposit Receipt — also called certificate of deposit, CF, term deposit, TDR. A certificate showing a deposit has been made at a bank or trust company, stating the amount, rate(s) of interest and repayment terms.

Depreciation — the decrease in the value of property because of wear and tear or obsolescence.

Dilution — this follows the sale by a company of shares from its treasury, which increases the number of shares outstanding and dilutes share profits and asset values because the total values have to be divided by the greater number of shares.

*Disability income insurance — provides specific, periodic payments to an individual totally disabled by accident or sickness.

Dividend — an amount designated by directors of a company for distribution to shareholders; a portion of earnings paid to shareholders as a return on their investment. Dividends are normally paid in cash but they can also be offered in the form of additional stock. A stock price that is quoted "cum dividend" includes payment of a declared dividend and is the time between the day the dividend is declared and the date of record (date on which all those recorded as holding the stock are listed to receive the dividend). A quote that is "ex dividend" does not include payment of a declared dividend because it is after the record date but before the date the dividend is paid.

*Dividend options — ways in which an owner can elect to receive policy dividends payable under participating life insurance. Typical choices: taking policy dividends in cash; using them to reduce premiums; converting them into paid-up additions to the sum insured; leaving them to accumulate as an interest-bearing cash deposit.

Dividend payable — dividend declared but not yet paid.

*Endorsement — provision changing the terms of an insurance contract.

*Endowment insurance — pays the face amount on a specified future date (maturity date) if the person insured is then living, or on death if that occurs sooner.

Equity — another term for common stock or, in real estate, the value built up in a property, including the down payment, the repayment of principal (the non-interest part of the mortgage) and any appreciation in market value.

*Extended term insurance — term insurance available as an option to the owner of a cash value life insurance policy who discontinues premium

payments. It continues the coverage for the face amount (less any outstanding policy loan) for a limited period of time, which depends on the cash value.

Face value — amount stated on the front of the policy to be paid on the death of the life insured.

Finance charge — total cost of getting a loan, including interest, loan fees, credit investigation fees; also, any interest due on a charge account.

Fixed-income security — any obligation, such as a bond, paying a stated interest rate for a stated period of time.

Floating rate note — a bond whose interest rate can vary.

Floor trader — a member of the stock exchange who makes trades on the floor of the exchange.

Front-end load — a commission or sales charge deducted from an investment in a mutual fund or savings plan before the rest of the money is invested.

Futures, futures market — contracts to buy/sell fixed amounts of certain commodities at a specified date in the future. Used by manufacturers and processors of raw materials as a hedge; by speculators for the purpose of making or losing large amounts of money.

Garnishment — a legal procedure allowing a lender to collect a portion of the wages of someone who is overdue in paying off a debt.

Going public — the process whereby a company meets the legal requirements to enable it to offer its shares for sale to the public.

Grace period — period, usually 30 or 31 days, after the premium due date on an insurance policy. During this time an overdue premium may be paid without penalty and the policy remains in effect.

Group life insurance — issued, usually without medical examination, on a group of people under a master contract.

Guaranteed insurability rider — provides the right to buy additional insurance on stated future dates without evidence of insurability.

Guaranteed Investment Certificate (GIC) — a term deposit, or a deposit certificate, usually issued by a trust company.

Guardian — the person named in your will to take responsibility for your minor children in the event of your death.

Hedge — a position taken in commodities or securities dealings to assure a sale or purchase at a future date at a specific price, or to counterbalance the sale or purchase of one commodity or security by buying or selling another.

Hedging — taking certain protective steps to minimize financial risk.

IDA, Investment Dealers' Association — an organization of Canadian investment dealers formed to maintain high ethical and financial standards within the investment businesses.

Incontestability — if the life insured dies after the first two years a policy has been in force, the company can't contest or refuse payment of the claim because of false statements in the application, unless they are fraudulent.

Insider — someone, usually a senior officer or director of a company, or an associate, who may be in a position to know about a company's plans or its financial position before that information is available to the public investors.

Inspection report — report completed by a consumer-reporting agency on behalf of an insurance company. Used to evaluate information in an insurance application as well as potential areas of concern other than health or occupation.

Installment loan — a set amount borrowed for a set period, to be repaid in regular monthly payments.

Insurability — acceptability of an applicant for insurance.

Insurance — an arrangement by which a risk is transferred to an insured.

Insurer — insurance company issuing the policy.

Interest — payment for the use of money.

Invest — purchase a stock for its underlying merits, with the intention of retaining it for income and growth over a long period of time.

Irrevocable beneficiary — beneficiary who can't be replaced without his/her consent. Consent is also necessary if the owner wishes to assign or surrender a policy or take a policy loan.

Joint and (last) survivor life annuity — annuity providing periodic payments lasting as long as either one of the two named people is alive.

Lapse — termination of a policy when premiums have not been paid.

193

Level premium insurance — premium does not change from year to year. It exceeds cost of protection in the earlier years and is less in later years. The excess paid in earlier years builds up a reserve which is invested and helps keep the amount of the premium down.

Leverage — using mostly borrowed money to make an investment.

Liabilities — what you owe, including charge account balances, rent, taxes, mortgages, personal loans, and so on.

Lien — a creditor's legal claim against a house or other property.

Life insured — person on whose death or disability insurance becomes payable.

Life underwriter — agent.

Limited payment life insurance — "whole life insurance," but premiums are payable only for a limited number of years.

Line of credit — maximum amount you can borrow on a credit card without getting special approval from the bank or department store.

Liquidity — the ability to convert your assets into cash quickly.

Listed stock — shares "listed" for active trading on a stock exchange.

Load, no-load, front-end load — a load is an acquisition fee for a mutual fund. Some have no fee; others, with a front-end load, take the fee from the first-year contributions to a fund.

Long — the state of owning securities.

Margin buying — using stock you already own as collateral to borrow from your stockbroker in order to finance additional stock purchases.

The Market — a term applying to a trading centre for securities or to the securities industry itself.

Market value — what an asset would bring in a sale between two disinterested parties in the open market.

Money market — generally, the market on which short-term debt securities are bought and sold.

Money-market fund — a mutual fund that invests only in short-term securities, such as treasury bills and bank certificates of deposit.

Morbidity rate — relative incidence of sickness or accidents in a given group of people during a given period of time.

194

Mortality rate — relative number of deaths in a given group of people during a given period of time.

Mortgage — a loan to buy a real-estate property, backed by the property.

Mortgage life insurance — insurance bought specifically to pay off the outstanding balance of a mortgage on the death of the insured.

Municipal bond — a bond issued by a local government.

MURB — Multiple Unit Residential Building. Apartments or condominium units meeting certain requirements and having potential tax advantages.

Mutual funds — a fund that pools individuals' money to invest in stocks or bonds or mortgages or gems, and so on.

Mutual life insurance company — a life insurance company without shareholders. Management is directed by an elected board.

Net worth — total assets minus total liabilities.

No-fault insurance — car insurance that pays your medical claims, but usually not damage to your car, regardless of who caused the accident.

No-load fund — a mutual fund that does not impose a sales charge.

Non–forfeiture options — choices available to a policy owner who discontinues premium payments on a policy that has accumulated a cash value. Policy owner can take value in cash, apply it to buy reduced paid-up insurance, or extended term insurance or use it as security for a loan against the policy to pay premium or premium dues.

No par value stock — shares with no specified nominal value.

Non-participating life insurance — policy owners do not share in any surplus earnings distributed by the company; no policy dividends are payable; premiums are set as closely as possible to the expected cost of insurance with a small margin for profit.

Odd lot — trading of a block of stock smaller than a board lot, which is the usual size. Normally, 100 shares constitutes a board lot.

Option — device used to speculate or hedge in securities markets. Buying a call option gives an investor the right to buy 100 shares of a stock at a certain price within a specified time; selling

195

a call option allows an investor to sell a stock under the same conditions.

Over-the-counter — the informal market for trading stocks not listed on stock exchanges.

*Participating life insurance — policy owners share in the surplus earnings distributed by the company through policy dividends. The premium is based on an estimate of future costs at a somewhat higher level and earnings at a somewhat lower level than the company feels likely to occur.

*Permanent life insurance — includes whole life insurance and endowment insurance and so is another name for cash value life insurance.

Record date — used for dividend payment purposes; the date chosen by directors of a company to determine the shareholders to whom a dividend is to be paid.

*Reduced paid-up insurance — insurance for a reduced amount, available as an option to the owner of a cash value life insurance policy who discontinues premium payments. It continues the coverage under the original policy for a reduced amount which depends on the cash value.

*Reinstatement — a policy that has lapsed may be reinstated within two years of the date of the lapse unless it has been surrendered for cash or one of the options of the reduced paid-up or extended term insurance has been exercised. Reinstatement requires payment of overdue premiums, satisfactory evidence of insurability and sometimes payment of any outstanding policy loan.

*Renewable term insurance — may be renewed when it expires without providing evidence of insurability. At each renewal date, every year or every five years, the premiums increase. There is usually a limit on the number of renewals, or else a limiting age, such as 65 or 70.

*Rescission right — right provided in many life insurance contracts whereby policy owner can cancel policy within a stated period, usually ten days. All premiums paid are refunded.

Reverse split — consolidation of existing shares into a smaller number of shares.

RHOSP — Registered Home Ownership Savings Plan, permitting tax-free savings for a down payment on a house. The plan must abide by government rules and regulations.

Rider — benefit attached to a policy providing extra amounts or types of coverage in addition to the basic policy benefits.

Right — issued by a company to existing shareholders, entitling them to buy additional shares at a specified price over a specified period in proportion to the number of shares they may have.

RRIF — a Registered Retirement Income Fund; a non-annuity investment vehicle for maturing RRSPs.

RRSP — Registered Retirement Savings Plan, which permits tax deferred savings for retirement purposes.

Safekeeping — custodial holding for securities owned by a customer of a stockbroker, trust company or bank.

SEC, Securities and Exchange Commission — the U.S. government agency which regulates and polices the U.S. securities industry and Canadian securities owned by or offered to U.S. residents.

Settlement date — the date on which a brokerage customer is required by regulation to pay his account or supply the security sold.

Settlement options — the ways policy owners or beneficiaries may choose to have policy benefits paid, other than payments in one sum.

Share — 1. one of the equal parts into which each class of the capital of a limited company is divided; 2. a certificate evidencing ownership of shares.

Share profit — a company's total profit available for common shares divided by the number of shares outstanding. Share profit in relation to the price of stock is a prime determinant of investment value.

Share warrant, stock purchase warrant — a certificate giving the holder the privilege of buying more stock at a specified price for a specified period of time.

Short selling — a strategy that involves borrowing stock and selling it on the market in the hope the price will go down, at which point an equal number of shares can be bought more cheaply and returned to the lender.

Single premium insurance — the entire premium is paid in one sum at the beginning of the policy.

Spot price — a current or cash price, usually for a commodity.

Stock life insurance company — company with share capital

197

in which management is directed by a board of directors elected partly by the shareholders and partly by the participating policy holders, if any.

Stock option — as an incentive for managers to perform well, the company gives them options to buy company shares at prices usually below the market level for specific periods of time.

Stock split — a division of the number of shares a company has outstanding, thereby increasing the total but not affecting proportionate ownership. Usually done to increase marketability — making more, lower-priced shares available for trading.

Stop-loss order — instruction to a broker to sell a stock if it falls to a certain level.

*Surrender — cancelling or giving up a policy to the insurance company in return for the cash surrender value or other nonforfeiture values.

Tax shelter — an investment that by government regulation can be made with untaxed or partly taxed dollars, including RRSPs, RHOSPs, Canadian films and some real estate, resource and research and development investments.

*Term insurance — provides protection for only a certain period unless renewable.

Trading date — the day on which a stock market transaction takes place.

TSE — Toronto Stock Exchange

*Underwriting — classifying the insurance risk of the applicant. It involves evaluating factors affecting the likelihood of death or sickness such as age, sex, health, occupation, hobbies, sports and lifestyle, so that an appropriate premium can be determined. Very few, only about 2 per cent of all applicants, represent such high risk that they are not insurable.

Underwriting — an undertaking from an investment dealer to sell shares of a company to investors and ensure that the proceeds of a complete sale are given to the company or group selling the shares, even if not all are sold. In a primary distribution, treasury shares are sold and the underwriting proceeds go to the company. A secondary distribution is the sale of existing stock from one group of shareholders to others.

*Variable annuity — an annuity in which the level of the income payments is not fixed

198

in advance, but depends on the investment performance of a specified fund in which the premiums have been placed.

Vesting — after a certain period, an employer's contributions to an employee's pension plan become locked in or vested.

VSE — Vancouver Stock Exchange

Waiver of premium — provides that insurance premiums do not have to be paid if the policy owner has been totally disabled for a certain period of time, usually six months.

Warrant — an option to buy the shares of a company within a certain period of time at a certain price.

Whole life insurance — provides protection for the lifetime of the person insured. Also known as ordinary or straight life insurance.

Yield — the amount of interest or dividend paid on a loan or an investment, expressed as a percentage.

Additional Reading

Books

Beach, Wayne, and Hepburn, Lyle. 1983. *Are You Paying Too Much Tax?* Toronto: McGraw-Hill Ryerson.

Brien, Mimi. 1982. *Money-Wise*. New York: Bantam Books.

Brown, J.J., and Ackerman, Jerry. 1982. *Start With $1000*. Toronto: Macmillan.

Chesler, Phyllis, and Goodman, Emily Jane. 1976. *Women, Money and Power*. New York: Bantam Books.

Delaney, Tom. 1983. *The Delaney Report on RRSPs*. Toronto: McGraw-Hill Ryerson.

Dickson, Paul. 1978. *The Official Rules*. New York: Delacorte Press.

———. 1980. *The Official Explanations*. New York: Delacorte Press.

Donoghue, William E. with Trilling, Thomas. 1983. *William E. Donoghue's No-Load Mutual Fund Guide*. New York: Harper & Row.

Fels, Lynn, 1981. *Living Together: Unmarried Couples in Canada*. Toronto: Personal Library.

Grainger, Alix. 1981. *Don't Bank On It*. New York: Doubleday.

Grenby, Mike. 1979. *Mike Grenby's Money Book*. Vancouver: International Self-Counsel Press.

————. 1979. *Mike Grenby's Tax Tips*. Vancouver: International Self-Counsel Press.

Knott, Leonard. 1982. *Before You Die*. Toronto: Personal Library.

Lakein, Alan. 1974. *How To Get Control of Your Time and Your Life*. New York: New American Library.

Lutner, Vernon E. 1979. *Meat Trade Secrets Exposed*. Vancouver: A. & F. Printing.

McDonald, M. 1978. *Legal First Aid*. Toronto: Coles Publishing.

Nelson, Paula. 1975. *The Joy of Money*. New York: Stein and Day.

Porter, Sylvia. 1983. *Sylvia Porter's New Money Book for the 80s*. New York: Doubleday.

Schumacher, E.F. 1975. *Small Is Beautiful*. New York: Harper & Row.

Smith, Charles W. 1981. *The Mind of the Market*. Totowa, N.J.: Rowman & Littlefield.

Snyder, Christopher. 1983. *How to Be Sure You Have the Right RRSP*. Toronto: Marpep Publishing.

————, and Anderson, Brian E., ed. 1979. *It's Your Money*. Toronto: Methuen.

Stewart, Walter. 1982. *Towers of Gold, Feet of Clay*. Toronto: Collins.

Swerd, Bonnie. 1983. *Count Your Change: A Woman's Guide to Sudden Financial Change*. Toronto: Fitzhenry and Whiteside.

Townson, Monica, and Stapenhurst, Frederick. 1982. *The Canadian Woman's Guide to Money*. Toronto: McGraw-Hill Ryerson.

Wylie, Betty Jane. 1982. *Beginnings: A Book for Widows*. Toronto: McClelland & Stewart.

————. 1982. *Encore: The Leftovers Cookbook*. Toronto: McClelland & Stewart.

Young, Fred J. 1983. *How To Get Rich and Stay Rich*. New York: Frederick Fell Publishers.

Zimmer, Henry B. 1982. *The New Canadian Tax and Investment Guide*. Toronto: Totem Books.

———— and Kaufman, Jeanne. 1982. *Reshaping Your Investment Strategies for the 1980s*. Toronto: Collins.

Pamphlets

Canadian Advisory Council on the Status of Women (Box 1541, Station B, Ottawa, Ontario K1P 5R5):

Five Million Women: A Study of the Canadian Housewife. Monique Proulx. June 1978.

Not How Many But How Few: Women Appointments to Boards, Commissions, Councils, Committees and Crown Corporations Within the Power of the Federal Government. Lyse Champagne. October 1980.

Pension Reform for Women: A Discussion Paper. December 1981.

Pension Reform with Women in Mind. Louise Dulude, May 1981.

The Second Time Around: A Study of Women Returning to the Work Force. Mary Pearson. April 1979.

Towards Equality for Women. 1983.

Women and Aging: A Report on the Rest of Our Lives. October 1978.

Women and Pensions. March 1982.

Women and Poverty: What Are Your Chances? March 1981.

Canadian Life and Health Insurance Association (Suite 2500, 20 Queen Street West, Toronto, Ontario M5H 3S2):

This Business of Life

A Buyer's Guide to Life Insurance

Family Money Manager: Budgeting Guide

Sharpen Your Pencil

Where Is Everything?

The Canadian Securities Institute (P.O. Box 225, Commerce Court South, Toronto, Ontario M5L 1E8; 1080 Beaver Hall Hill, Montreal 128, Quebec H2Z 1S8; or Box 49151, Three Bentall Centre, Vancouver, British Columbia.):

How To Invest in Canadian Securities

How To Invest Your Money

How To Read a Financial Statement

Investment Terms and Definitions

The Money Saver (Box 370, Bath, Ontario K0H 1G0):
monthly newsletter; $12 a year

National Council of Welfare (Brooke Claxton Building, Ottawa, Ontario K1A 0K9):

Women and Poverty

Index

AGF, 114
Alberta, 140, 141, 146, 155
Allowances, 60, 132, 134-35.
   See also Budget
American Council of Life
   Insurance, 74
American Express, 33, 35
Annuities, 80-81, 87-88
Antiques, 116-17
Assets, 12-16, 146-47; sterile,
   116-17

Bank accounts, 16, 29-30,
   37-38, 42, 63, 65, 88. *See
   also* Chequing accounts,
   Savings accounts
Banking machines, 42, 43-44
Bank of Canada, 65, 68-69
Bankruptcy, 165
Banks, 37, 39-40, 46-47, 58, 68
Barter, 168
Bell Canada, 108-9
Beneficiary, 76, 144
Bequests, 142, 144, 145
Billings, Victoria, *quoted*, 11

Bolton Tremblay, 114
Bonds, 64, 66. *See also* Canada
   Savings Bonds
Bonuses, 25, 67-68
Book clubs, 58
Borrowing, *see* Loans
Brecht, Bertolt, *quoted*, 24
British Columbia, 39-40, 99,
   140, 141, 146, 147
Brokerage houses, 93, 94,
   103-5; accounts with, 104-5;
   commissions, 111-12, 115;
   discount, 110-11
Budget, 9, 46, 51-62, 134-35
Bullion, 107
Butler, Samuel, *quoted*, 163

Canada Deposit Insurance Corp.
   (CDIC), 42-43
Canada Mortgage and Housing
   Corp., 123
Canada Pension Plan (CPP), 18,
   88, 146n.
Canada Savings Bonds (CSBs),
   10, 47-48, 63, 64-68, 88;

buying, 64; interest on, 16, 64, 67, 154-55
Canadian Bankers' Assoc., 42
Capital gains, 94-95, 97-98, 99-101, 108, 113, 145, 161
Capital losses, 97-98, 113, 145
Carte Blanche, 33
Cash, 9, 12, 34, 53, 63
Charge account, 30
Charge cards, 33
Chatelaine, 61
Cheque-book, 40-41, 160
Cheques, 34
Chequing accounts, 38
Chesler, Phyllis, 11
Children, 12, 16, 75, 77, 131-37, 143, 159
Chores, 132, 136
Churning, 104
Clothing, *see* Needs
Codecil, 142
Collateral, 33, 46, 48, 49, 64
Collectibles, 116-17
Commissions, 111-12, 115
Condominiums, 10, 120
Consumer Relations, Ministry of, 32
Consumers' Assoc. of Canada, 40
Co-op housing, 120
Credit, 9, 29-36, 45; bureaus, 30-31; cards, 29, 30, 33-36; limit, 35; rating, 9, 29-30; unions, 38, 43

Debts, 9-10, 32, 46, 53, 164-65; provincial assistance, 165
Deductions, income tax, 48, 70, 86, 108, 127-28, 155, 156n., 159, 160; payroll, 17-18
Delaney, Tom, 87

Dickson, Paul, *quoted*, 117
Discrimination, 32, 49
Dividends, 97, 98, 99-101, 155-57
Divorce, 7, 11, 32, 76, 98, 146; settlements, 76, 146-48
Doll's House, 11
Dominion Securities Ames, Ltd., 100
Dowling, Constance, 27
Down payment, *see* Housing, buying of
Dulude, Louise, *quoted*, 146-47

Education, 56, 75, 136-37, 142
Emergency fund, 63, 77
Encore: The Leftovers Cookbook, 59, 60
Energy costs, 59
Estates, intestate, 140-41
Executor, 142, 143, 144
Expenses, 53-55, 57-62; final, 74-75; housing, 120-24; monthly, 135

Farms, 127-28
Fels, Lyn, 148
Filing system, 149-53
Financial planning, *see* Budget
Food, *see* Needs
Free-lance workers, 33
Friedan, Betty, 8
Fuller, Thomas, *quoted*, 71
Funeral expenses, 74-75, 76, 77, 78

Gems, 115
Getty, J. Paul, 15
Gifts, 16, 25, 133, 157-58
Gilbreth, Lillian, 58

Goals, 21-26, 53, 56-57, 136, 169
Godkewitsch, Michael, *quoted*, 22, 23
Grainger, Alix, *quoted*, 41
Gross up, 100
Guaranteed Income Supplements (GIS), 88-91
Guaranteed-investment certificates (GICs), 10, 16, 42, 63, 68
Guardian, 77, 143, 144
Guardian Capital, 114

Horses, 115-16
Household management, 58-62
Housing, buying of: 119-29; costs, 120-21; disadvantages, 123; down payment, 123, 125; inspection, 122; interim agreement, 122; second property, 126-27
Housing, selling of, 127, 129
Human Tissue Gift Act (Ont.), 146

Impulse buying, 57
Income, 8-9, 12, 25, 53, 121; discretionary, 18, 95, 96; gross, 16-17; from investments, 94, 109; net, 52; splitting, 157-60; tax, *see* Tax, income
Indexed Security Investment Plans (ISIPs), 113
Inflation, 84, 90, 109, 113
Inheritance, 75, 140-42
Insurance, 52, 73-82, 150; children and, 75, 78-79; disability, 79-80; group, 79; on income, 75, 76, 77; life,

76, 78, 80, 144-45; loans, 47-48, 79; medical, 80, 81; mortgage, 75, 76, 77, 144; premiums, 78-79, 80; property, 81-82
Interest, 47, 58, 97, 98, 99-101, 105; on bonds, 64, 65; on GICs/term-deposits, 68; rates, 114, 124; on RHOSPs, 70; on T-Bills, 69
Investing, 8, 94
Investment clubs, 102
Investments, 10, 64-69, 88, 93-117

Jefferson, Thomas, *quoted*, 168

Knott, Leonard, 146
Kome, Penney, *quoted*, 75

Lawyers, 93, 144, 147-48
Leacock, Stephen, 41
Legacies, 75
Lerner, Dr. Paul, 22
Lewis, Joe E., 22
Liabilities, 12-16
Limited editions, 116
Loans, 9, 45-49, 58, 64, 158; open, 46-47, 164; renegotiating, 48-49
Lotteries, 116
Lutner, Vernon, 59

McCubbin, Hamilton, 76
McLuhan, Marshall, *quoted*, 57-58
Maintenance costs, 58, 121, 126
Manitoba, 126, 140, 141, 146, 147
Marriage, 7, 11, 25-26, 27, 30, 32, 64, 75, 126, 140

Marriage contracts, 26, 147, 148
Maslow, Abraham, 24
MasterCard, 33, 41, 43, 44
Memorial societies, 145
Money-market funds, 114
Mortgages, 10, 13, 113-14, 120, 121, 123-25, 144; blanket, 120; first, 123; insurance on, 75, 76, 77; interest rates on, 124; open, 125; second, 123, 124
Mortgage Insurance Co. of Canada, 123
Motherhood, *see* Parenthood
Mutual funds, 114-15

Nash, Ogden, *quoted*, 28
National Council of Welfare, *see Women and Poverty*
Needs, 24, 52, 58-61
Nelson, Paula, *quoted*, 9
Net-worth statement, 12-16, 46, 84, 144
New Brunswick, 140, 141
Newfoundland, 140, 141
Noble, Winifred, *quoted*, 94
Nova Scotia, 140, 141

Oates, Joyce Carol, *quoted*, 98
Old Age Security (OAS), 9, 88, 90-91
Ontario, 100-101, 140, 141, 145-46
Outgo, 17-18, 52, 53-54
Overdraft protection, 41

Parenthood, 8, 11, 12, 131-37
Penny stocks, 115
Pensions, 81, 84-85; employer-sponsored, 85-86, 88, 146-47. *See also* Canada Pension

Plan, Old Age Security
Portfolios, 64, 88, 93, 102-3, 107-17
Poverty, 7, 12, 23, 26-27, 91
Poverty line, 7, 9, 75, 88
Prime rate, 10, 49
Prince Edward Island, 140, 141, 145, 146
Priorities, *see* Goals
Promissory notes, 158
Property taxes, *see* Tax, property
Provincial income supplements, 89
Psychology Today, 18

Quebec, 140, 141, 143, 144-45, 146, 155-56
Quebec Pension Plan, 88, 146n.

Recipes for a Small Planet, 59
Registered Home Ownership Plan (RHOSP), 42, 69-71
Registered Retirement Income Fund (RRIF), 87-88
Registered Retirement Savings Plan (RRSP), 11, 42, 85-87, 88, 159
Rental property, 123, 127-28
Retirement income, 75, 77, 84-91
Revenue Canada, 70, 158, 160; Taxation, 69
Robertson, James, *quoted*, 169
Roher, Martin, 22
Royal Commission on the Status of Women (1970), 169
Runyon, Damon, *quoted*, 139

Safety-deposit boxes, 43, 107, 149-50

Saskatchewan, 140, 141, 146
Saving, 133, 167-68
Savings, 52, 56, 63-71
Savings accounts, daily-interest, 33-34, 37-38, 39, 54; premium, 37
Self-employed persons, 80
Separation, 32
Service charges, 34, 38, 39-40
Shares, *see* Stocks
Shaw, George Bernard, *quoted*, 131
Sheehy, Gail, *quoted*, 33
Shelter, *see* Needs
Single-parent families, 12, 76-77, 163-64
Single women, 7, 26-27, 32, 77-78, 129, 142
Snyder, Christopher, 87
Stein, Gertrude, *quoted*, 18-19
Stock market, 93, 102, 115
Stocks, 88, 98, 102-3, 108-12, 155-57; blue-chip, 95; common, 108-9, 113; new issues, 110-11; penny, 115; preferred, 108, 109-10, 157
Stone, Olive, *quoted*, 146-47
Succession duties, 144-45
Survivor benefits, 81, 88

Tax: deductions, 48, 86, 108, 127-28, 155, 156n., 159, 160; dividend credit, 48, 97, 98-101, 108, 155-57; income, 48, 87, 97-99, 149-61;

property, 53, 120; withholding, 87
Tax shelters, 153
Term-deposits, 16, 42, 68
This Business of Life, 80
Toronto Star, 75
Toronto Stock Exchange, 110-12
Treasury Bills, 63, 68-69
Trust, irrevocable, 142
Trust companies, 38, 42, 68, 142
Tucker, Sophie, *quoted*, 12, 78

Unions, 80
United States, 12
Utility bills, 44, 61-62

Vancouver Stock Exchange, 115
Victoria, B.C., 31
Visa, 33, 34-35, 41, 43, 44

Wages, 8, 26
Warranties, 122
Widowhood, 7, 9, 10, 11, 21, 32, 150
Wills, 139-45
Winnipeg, 44
Women and Poverty, 7, 8, 26, 27, 77
Working women, 75, 76-77, 126
Writs, 30-31
Wylie, Betty Jane, 59

Yukon, 146

Acknowledgements

Special thanks to Gordon Bonn of Dominion Securities Ames in Toronto and to Elizabeth Skinner of Royal Trust in Victoria for background information, facts and figures; to my daughter Avon MacFarlane of Toronto, who typed one version of the manuscript, making sense out of scratches and scrawls added to typed sheets; to friends and family members who made suggestions; to the women of Victoria who first showed me the need for this book; and to class participants who asked the questions and who shared the experiences that helped me to shape it.

Thanks, too, for the invaluable help and expertise of our editor, Jennifer Glossop, and for Betty Jane's friendship, which survived the problems of co-authors writing a book while living three thousand miles apart.

And grateful thanks to my husband and best friend, Don MacFarlane, and to our son Scott MacFarlane (who happened to be at home at the time the book was being written) for all their encouragement, patience, loving support, prepared dinners and even breakfasts in a paper-strewn bed!

LYNNE MACFARLANE

And I would like to thank Bruce Powe and Isabel Wegg at the Canadian Life and Health Insurance Association and Lucy Greene at Sun Life for their generosity with their knowledge and assistance, as well as my favourite editor, Jennifer Glossop, and Lynne, for her tolerance and patience.

BETTY JANE WYLIE